An Historical Guide to

Landmarks, Events, Activities, Parks, Beaches, Plants & Wildlife, Accommodations, Restaurants, Shops & Services

PeNder

ISLaNds

By V.A. Lindholm

Hidden Lighthouse Publishers
Canadian Rockies/Vancouver/Victoria

PuBLicatioN INFoRMatioN

Hidden Lighthouse Publishers
A division of Diskover Office Software Ltd.
575 Fernhill Rd
Site 3, Comp. 4
Mayne Island, BC V0N 2J0

Extreme care has been taken to ensure that all information presented in this book is accurate and up-to-date, and neither the author nor the publisher can be held responsible for any errors.

Cover design, page design and composition by Vicky Lindholm
All photos, with the exception of those listed under Credits, by Vicky Lindholm
Maps by Vicky Lindholm

Front cover photo:
   A sunset, the Pender Islands
Back cover photo:
   The canal, the Pender Islands

To Ken
who spent hours hiking the darkest
of dark forests and climbing the
tallest of tall mountains to get me
just the right shot

Contents

Contents

A Tale of the Penders

Port Washington

It was in the mid-1880's when an Englishman, named Washington Grimmer, purchased a herd of cattle from one of the southern Gulf Islands...

In a one-day cattle drive, Washington single-handedly drove his herd of cattle across the Island and hauled them onto the deck of a schooner by their horns. When the schooner reached the bay near his home, he lowered the cattle into the water and towed each one of them ashore in the darkness.[1]

Washington Grimmer was born in the 1850's and immigrated to Canada with his family. In the 1880's, he crawled out of the window of a ship with his gun and dog, and set out for the Pender Islands.[2]

The ambitious Washington Grimmer was an ardent builder, having constructed several homes on North Pender.[3] With the help of his brother-in-law, he built the road that connects the two wharves.[4]

In the early 1890's, Washington became **the Postman** for the Pender Islands, operating the post office from a home he had built there.[5] He was eventually made Justice of the Peace.[6]

Years later, his eldest son had this to say about him:

"...being of the restless type, he always found lots to do – a quick, wiry little man with a quick temper which, like a storm in a teapot, was over in minutes."
Neptune Grimmer[7]

PeNder ISLaNdS

THiNgS to KNoW

Just sit right back and you'll hear a tale…

Pender is a pristine island in the southern Gulf Islands. It lies in the rain shadow of the Vancouver Island Mountains, which protects it from storms that blow in from the Pacific Ocean. Often referred to as the *Banana Belt* of Canada, the Islands have a Mediterranean-type climate, which is warm during the day and cool at night.

Pender Island enjoys an average of 2,000 hours of sunshine, annually. With the longest frost-free season in the country, spring begins as early as February. Because it rarely snows, a winter weekend on Pender can be quite cozy with some logs on a *paia* (fire).

At 34 sq km, Pender is one of the largest of the southern Gulf Islands. Its rolling hills and roads are reminiscent of an English *Illahee* (countryside). There

are no traffic lights, no curbs and no sidewalks, making it quite a quaint attraction.

Most of the Gulf Islands are uninhabited. However, at the time of this writing, Pender had a population of about 2,200 permanent residents. Its population consists mainly of young families, retirees and business professionals.

Part-time residents own cottages as their 'home away from home', living as *weekenders* (people who spend weekends on Pender) during the tourist season. At that time, the population swells to around 4,000.

Pender Island is separated by a canal into two, small islands known as *North Pender* and *South Pender*. North Pender provides most of the facilities. South Pender is more *illahee* (rural).

The two islands are, together, locally referred to as *the Penders* and a friendly rivalry has always existed between them.[8] Because of the nationalities of the people who originally settled there, North and South Pender were referred to as *Little Scotland* and *Little England*.[9]

NoɾtH PeNdeɾ ISLaNd WHaɾveS

In 1890, the first wharf was built, on the northwest side of North Pender. It accommodated ships coming through the waterway called *Swanson Channel*. The port was named *Port Washington*, in honor of **the Postman**.[10]

Port Washington Wharf in 1925 – Pender Islands Museum

At the turn of the century, another wharf was built, in a bay called *Hope Bay*.[11] Because it was located on the opposite side of North Pender, a rivalry began between the largely English community of Port Washington and the Scottish community of Hope Bay.[12]

Hope Bay wharf in 1946
Pender Islands Museum

In the early 1950's, the ship named *Princess Elaine* was introduced to the waters surrounding the Gulf Islands. The Port Washington wharf was the only wharf in the outer Gulf Islands that could accommodate it.[13]

Today, the Port Washington wharf is used to transport schoolchildren to neighboring schools, and by sea planes traveling between Pender and *Big Smoke* (Vancouver).

Occasionally, freighters can be seen at the Hope Bay wharf, waiting their turn to proceed to larger ports of call.

PeNder ISLaNdS PoSt OFFice

Initially, **the Postman** would row to Mayne Island to collect the mail.[14] When the Port Washington wharf was built in the 1890's, a steamer ship began delivering it directly to the wharf.[15]

That same year, **the Postman** built a small cabin on his farm nearby and converted part of the porch into a mailroom, from which he provided postal service.[16] The cabin was enlarged at the turn of the century.[17] Today, it is a private residence on an old orchard.

A year or so after **the Postman** accepted his postal duties, the post office was moved to a small building at the head of the Hope Bay wharf. The mail came in by way of an overland trail and the settlers would stand and wait at a little counter for their envelopes and parcels to be dispatched.[18]

A few years later, the first store on the Penders was built near the Hope Bay wharf. Named *Corbett's*,[19] the small frame building soon became the home of the *Pender Island Post Office*. The address was simply 'Pender Island'.[20]

Pender Island Post Office in 1933
Hope Bay Rising Holdings Ltd.

In 1910, another store was built, at the head of the first wharf. It was named the *General Store*, and the *Port Washington Post Office* was established there.[21] Its address was 'Port Washington'.[22]

Port Washington Post Office, early 1900's
BC Archives D-08531

Soon, Corbett's store at Hope Bay was moved into a new building that had been constructed nearby. The Pender Island Post Office was then relocated to a large area at the back of the new store.[23] Each time the store changed hands the new owners continued to use **the Postman's** original post office box in the post office.[24]

Much later, in the 1970's, the two post offices were consolidated as the *Pender Islands Post Office* and were moved into a mall in the center of North Pender. Within a decade, both stores had closed.[25]

A few years prior to this writing, the store at Hope Bay was restored.[26] The buildings are now being operated as offices, a gift store and a café.

Pender Island Post Office
as it appears today

Although the General Store at Port Washington changed owners several times, it was home to the Port Washington Post Office for over 70 years.[27]   At the time of this writing, it was also being restored.

**Port Washington Post Office
as it appears today**

Today, the Pender Islands Post Office sits behind the mall to which it had been moved in the 1970's. It serves both North and South Pender.

PeNdeɾ ISLaNdS CoMMuNity HaLL

The first community hall to be built on North Pender was constructed in the 1880's, on land owned by the man who would later become **the Postman**.[28] The hall sat midway between Port Washington and Hope Bay.[29]

In the year 1910, a second community hall was built,[30] beside Corbett's store at Hope Bay. It was called the *Hope Bay Community Hall*. Unfortunately, the hall was built on uneven ground, which caused its post foundation to become unstable.[31]

Two years later, the builder of the General Store leased some of his land for a third community hall, called the *Port Washington Community Hall*. It replaced the first hall in that community,[32] which had been disposed of at the turn of the century.[33]

By 1912, there were two halls in operation on North Pender; the Port Washington Community Hall and the Hope Bay Community Hall.[34]

The Port Washington hall was initially a square box. It had a flat roof that was later replaced with a peaked roof. Because it had no electricity or indoor plumbing, water had to be brought in to the hall and gas lanterns were hung from the ceiling for light.[35]

For a while, the Port Washington hall was used as a school and for holding church services. A year after it was built, roller-skating was introduced to it and, soon, the floor became so uneven that dancing proved impossible and a new floor had to be laid.[36]

In the 1930's, some residents stayed up until midnight planning the Islands' first fall fair. It was hosted at the Hope Bay Community Hall and its fair grounds.[37]

By the 1960's, the post foundation supporting the Hope Bay hall had deteriorated, causing it to be razed by fire.[38] Subsequently, it was torn down and the Port Washington hall became the social center for the Penders.[39]

Port Washington Community Hall in 1963 - Pender Islands Museum

Unfortunately, a decade later, the Port Washington hall was also razed by fire.[40] When its remains were torn down, its assets were transferred to a new school that had just been built in the center of the Island. The plans for the school had included a hall. It was the fourth hall to be built on the Penders.[41]

Recently, a fifth community hall was built on North Pender, on Bedwell Harbour Road.[42]

Under the guidance of a Tsimshian carver, a project was undertaken by about 60 women to carve three poles that now stand at the entrance to the new hall. The poles, called the Women's Unity Welcome Poles, display the figures of mother bears and a bear cub.[43]

Today, the *Pender Islands Community Hall* and its fair grounds are host to the *Pender Islands Farmer's Market* and the *Pender Islands Fall Fair*.

Visitors to the Island can bring their *tillicum* (friends) to the hall and enjoy a variety of other civic functions, from musìcal concerts to performing arts presentations.

PeNdeř ISLaNdS SCHOOL

In the 1890's, **the Postman** and two other settlers chose a teacher for the children of North Pender. Classes were held on his property, in the Port Washington Community Hall.[44]

The hall was equipped with a painted blackboard, tables and benches. Students carried a lard pail lunch and their own textbooks to class, and completed their assignments on slates.[45]

The following year, a small outbuilding was built beside the hall. When it was equipped with desks, classes were then moved there from the hall. Water was carried to the building from the spring and a student was paid to stoke a fire for heat.[46]

At the turn of the century, the settlers decided that a new school was needed. Reportedly, they drew a circle around a map of North Pender and marked the building site in the centre, at Hope Bay.[47]

Upon completion of the school at Hope Bay, one of the families living on the Island made a home out of the old buildings at Port Washington.[48]

At the end of the first school year, 23 students wrote the high school entrance examinations. Of the four students who passed the exams, two attended the school at Hope Bay.[49] As a result, its teacher became well known in educational circles around British Columbia.[50]

At that time, the school consisted of only one room on a single level. Eventually, the front entrance was moved to the side of the building and a second level was added.[51]

Hope Bay School in 1946 - Pender Islands Museum

In the 1970's, a third school was built on North Pender. It was named the *Pender Islands Elementary Secondary School.*[52]

When construction of the new school was complete, the old schoolhouse at Hope Bay was sold to the Recreation and Agriculture Hall Association for one dollar.[53] It is now home to a thrift store.

Hope Bay School as it appears today

PeNder ISLaNdS

Today, the Pender Islands Elementary Secondary School, which is located on Canal Road, serves the communities of both North and South Pender. It accommodates over 100 full-time equivalent students, some of whom are transported to schools on neighboring Islands by the *Scholar Ship* (a water taxi that carries school children).

PeNder ISLaNdS PubLic LibrarY

In the 1940's, a very small library operated from within the General Store at Port Washington. The library functioned from inside the store for more than two decades.[54]

In the early 1970's, a woman who had a large book collection decided to share them. When she approached a church on the Island, they agreed to let her store her books in a small room at the back of the church building. A few months later, a library was opened there. It was called the *Pender Lender*.[55]

Initially, only a few book borrowers came into the library. However, when the staff purchased 13 new books to add to their collection of used books, more borrowers started to show interest. Eventually, the library began receiving books from The Canada Council.[56]

The church room had an unreliable oil furnace. Whenever it malfunctioned, the library staff had to wear their coats and gloves to keep warm.[57] So when the new school was built a few years later, the staff moved the library into a small building on the old school grounds at Hope Bay. When they put child-sized furniture in a corner, even children started visiting the library.[58]

In 1990, an architect designed a new building next door, in which to house the library. The building was named the *Auchterlonie Center*.[59] When the library moved into the new building, the little building on the old school grounds became home to a playschool.

PeNder IsLands

Today, the *Pender Islands Public Library*, which is still jokingly referred to as the Pender Lender, is the Penders' fourth library. Located on Bedwell Harbour Road, it is home to 13,000 books and enjoys the highest percentage of per capita support for rural libraries in all of British Columbia.[60]

Driftwood Centre

In the late 1970's, a couple built a mall in the center of North Pender. In its construction, they counted and laid over 24,000 bricks by hand.[61]

Today, the *Driftwood Centre*, which is locally referred to as *The Drift*, is home to a variety of businesses. At the time of this writing, they included a post office, liquor store, drugstore, laundromat, bank and bakery, as well as a grocery store and gift stores.

You can also gas up your *chikchik* (wagon) at the service station there. The center is located on Bedwell Harbour Road.

Magic Lake Market

The *Magic Lake Market* supplies the surrounding community with groceries and movie rentals. It is located on Schooner Way.

Southridge Farms Country Store

The *Southridge Farms Country Store* provides for fresh produce, groceries, coffee and pastries. It is located on Port Washington Road.

RCMP Station

Before the turn of the century, rum running, hi-jacking, sheep stealing and wool smuggling were common occurrences on the Penders. The sheep farmers were all too familiar with a mysterious little smuggler from the U.S. who wore a very, very tall hat.[62]

Known locally as 'Old Burke', the smuggler would pay the farmers for their wool fleeces,[63] which they would store for him in their barns. Then, once a year, at dusk, the little smuggler's big black boat would glide silently into the harbours. In the morning, the sheep fleeces, which had been carefully rolled up by the farmers, would be gone.[64]

Years later, when statistics showed that a tiny island had become the largest wool distributor in Washington State, the authorities became suspicious. So, to set a trap for the smuggler, they marked some fleeces that were stored in a shed at the harbour.[65]

Eventually, the marked fleeces were found in the possession of Old Burke, who was promptly arrested.[66] One of the farmers went to court to defend him and, subsequently, the smuggler was acquitted.[67] Nevertheless, wool smuggling ceased with the arrest of the night visitor in the tall, tall hat.[68]

Today, there are over 6,000 *Queen's Cowboys* (RCMP) employed in British Columbia. However, there is only one Corporal stationed at the two-person RCMP detachment on North Pender. He is in charge of law enforcement for all of the outer Gulf Islands. The station is located on Bedwell Harbour Road.

The RCMP boat can often be seen docked at one of the government wharves.

PeNder IsLaNds Fire aNd ReScUe

Because fires had destroyed so many buildings on the Penders in the first half of the century, they were incorporated into a fire protection district in the 1970's[69] and the *Pender Islands Volunteer Fire Brigade* was formed.[70]

The fire brigade consisted of a *high muckymuck* (fire chief), two crew heads and 14 *smoke eaters* (fire fighters). Their equipment consisted of four shovels, and a four-wheel drive power wagon that had a small pump in the front and a 1500 liter water tank in the back.[71]

Soon, a fire hall was built on North Pender, on land that had previously been used as a skeet shooting area by the Rod and Gun Club. That year, the society purchased a new fire truck and a fire siren. They were followed by a

tanker truck the next year. In the 1980's, the *South Pender Fire Hall* was opened on South Pender.[72]

A decade later, a second hall was built on North Pender.[73] Today, there are a total of three fire halls on North Pender.

In the year prior to this writing, the *Pender Islands Fire and Rescue* acquired a new fire truck. Specially designed to provide fire protection to a large resort, it services the fire hall on South Pender.

PeNder ISLaNdS

BiSHop CoLeMaN HeaLtH CeNter

Reportedly, there was no qualified medical aid in the outer Gulf Islands until the turn of the century. Around that time, a physician opened a practice on neighboring Salt Spring Island. He would row to the Penders whenever he was needed.[74]

The first resident doctor to serve the Penders set up his practice during World War I. Several other physicians provided medical aid during the 1920's, either as visiting doctors or as residents.[75] Much later, in the 1960's, the Royal Canadian Legion developed a medical clinic as a centennial project.[76]

In the 1980's, the *Bishop Coleman Memorial Health Centre* was built, followed by an ambulance center a decade later.[77]

Today, the health center, which is located on Canal Road, offers medical and dental facilities. An optometrist and physiotherapist also have offices there.

In addition, the Pender Islands provide for chiropractic, massage therapy, acupuncture, Reiki, and other healing and preventive alternatives.

PeNder ISLaNdS VeteriNary CLiNic

The *Pender Island Veterinary Clinic, on Cutlass Court*, is a full-service veterinary hospital. It provides quality medical and surgical veterinary care.

PeNder ISLaNd GoLF & CoUNtry CLUb

In the 1930's, the son of **the Postman** owned a sheep pasture in a valley. One day, he and his siblings decided to develop it into a golf course.[78]

Over time, six people purchased the land so they could improve the course. They formed a golf club, and worked hard at the tees. They set up the holes, cutting the greens with a push-type lawnmower.

Initially, the golfers climbed down a ladder at the sixth hole. The club members later built steps there.[79]

On the pasture was a small two-room cabin, which the club members converted into a clubhouse. Much later, in the 1980's, a new clubhouse was built.[80]

Today, the *Pender Island Golf and Country Club* has over 350 members. The challenging, 9-hole RCGA and CLGA rated course has several different tee areas and plays as an 18-hole par 68 for men and par 69 for women. The *New Year's Golf Tournament* is an event held at the golf and country club each year.

Open year-round, the course, which is located on Shoal Road, provides for a well-equipped golf shop. Power carts, pull carts and golf clubs are available for rent. Volunteers recently contributed over 6,000 hours constructing a network of golf cart paths out of driftwood.[81]

GoLF IsLaNd DiSc ParK

In the 1980's, a few residents of the Penders laid out a special golf course near the center of the Island.[82] Three years later, the *British Columbia Provincial Disc Golf Tournament* was held at the course.

Today, the *Golf Island Disc Park* is the only golf park of its kind in the Gulf Islands, where 'frisbee golf' has become a popular, year-round sport.

Rated as one of the top five in North America, the frisbee golf course is set up with various hoops and obstacles. Par on the front nine is 27 and par on the back nine is 29. Use of the course is free, but players are required to bring their own frisbees.

Each year, the park hosts the annual *Pender Island Invitational Disc Tournament.* The tournament attracts players from the entire West Coast of North America. The park is located on Galleon Way.

Places to Stay

In the 1920's, a family built an impressive house across from the General Store at Port Washington. They ran the house as a hotel, called *Grosvenor House.* The hotel was destroyed by fire in the 1940's.[83]

Today, most of the accommodations on the Pender Islands are located on North Pender. Many of the old Inns and lodges are still in operation and, along with some other accommodations, have been listed in this book.

Prior Centennial Campground

Set in the shade of a thick forest, *Prior Centennial Provincial Campground* provides for 17 campsites on the southeast side of North Pender. The campground is located on Bedwell Harbour Road. Reservations are recommended. Phone: 1-800-689-9025

Oaks Bluff Lodge

Oaks Bluff Lodge is an Inn on the southern shore of North Pender. It is located on Pirates Road. Phone: 1-866-228-4397

Kingfisher Cove

Kingfisher Cove is a cottage rental on the northern shore of South Pender. It is located on Ainslie Point Road. Phone: (604) 228-8079

Clam Bay Farm Retreat

The *Clam Bay Farm Retreat* is a working farm that offers home and cottage rentals on the northeast side of North Pender. Phone: 1-877-662-3414

Beaumont Provincial Campground

Beaumont Provincial Campground is located in a marine park. It provides for 15 tent sites on the southern shore of South Pender. You can access the year-round sites by boat. You can also access them on foot, from the summit of Mount Norman, which is accessible by way of a trail on Canal Road.

Delia's Shangri-La Oceanfront B&B

Delia's Shangri-La Oceanfront Bed and Breakfast is a B&B on the southern shore of North Pender. It is located on Pirates Road. Phone: 1-877-629-2800

Arcadia By The Sea

In the 1940's, a lawyer purchased a 10-room, two-storey home on North Pender. The home was originally named *Mille Fleurs*.

Soon, the lawyer's wife decided to remodel the interior of the home and convert it into a guest cottage. Because a friend supplied the bedrooms with Beautyrest® mattresses, she changed the name of the home to the *Beautyrest Lodge*. Two years later, she employed an agency to find guests for her lodge, and then opened it for business.[84]

Eventually, the woman added six more cottages, and hired an off-island crew to build a separate building with a dining room and lounge.[85] Subsequently, the lodge became one of the most popular resorts in all the Gulf Islands.[86]

After 27 successful years, the woman retired and the lodge was sold. New owners changed the name to *Otter Bay Lodge*.[87]

Arcadia By The Sea in 1955 - Pender Islands Museum

In the 1960's, the lodge was renamed *Pender Lodge*.[88] It boasted a licensed lounge and dining room, as well as sleeping and housekeeping cottages. There was also a swimming pool and tennis courts on the property.[89]

Today, the lodge is called *Arcadia By The Sea*. It is located on MacKinnon Road, on the northwest shore of North Pender. Phone: 1-877-470-8439

Arcadia By The Sea as it appears today

Beauty Rest By The Sea B&B

The *Beauty Rest By The Sea Bed and Breakfast* is a B&B on the northwest shore of North Pender. It is located on MacKinnon Road. Phone: (250) 629-3855

Sahhali Serenity Oceanfront B&B

The *Sahhali Serenity Oceanfront Bed and Breakfast* is a B&B on the southern shore of North Pender. Phone: 1-877-625-2583

Port Browning Marina Resort

Just before the outbreak of World War I, a settler arranged for a home to be built near a harbour on North Pender.[90]

> **Treasure Hunt**
> *There is a plaque, commemorating the effort taken to develop the golf course. Can you find it on the Penders?*

The Maples.[91]

In the 1920's, he built three cabins on the land, and he and his wife converted the property into a resort. Because there were large Maple trees on the property, they called the resort

Browning Harbour in 1946 - Pender Island Museum

The couple served meals to all of their guests and, over time, the Maples became one of North Pender's most popular resorts.[92]

The resort operated for more than 40 years, before closing in the 1970's.[93] The home and one of the cabins can still be seen from Browning Harbour today.

The year-round *Port Browning Marina Resort* offers self-contained cabins near the old resort on Browning Harbour, as well as camping for tents, trailers and campervans. A tennis court and swimming pool are also available.

The *Port Browning Marina* provides for temporary boat anchorage at the harbour. The resort and marina are located on Hamilton Road. Phone: (250) 629-3493

THe TiMbers

The Timbers is a resort offering cottage and cabin rentals on the southern shore of North Pender. The resort, which is located on Shark Road, provides for a private dock. Phone: 1-866-472-7982

CaMeLot By THe Sea B&B

Camelot By The Sea is a B&B on the northwest shore of North Pender. It is located on Otter Bay Road. Phone: (250) 629-370

OceaNSide INN

The *Oceanside Inn* is a country Inn on the northeastern shore of North Pender. It is located on Armadale Road. Phone: 1-800-601-3284

EateNtoN HoUSe Bed & BreaKFast INN

The *Eatenton House Bed and Breakfast Inn* is a B&B on the southeast side of North Pender. It is located on Scarff Road. Phone: 1-888-780-9994

Corbett House B&B

At the turn of the century, the settler who would eventually open the first store on the Penders moved with his family to North Pender.[94]

The following year, he purchased some land on the northeast side of North Pender. There, he established a farm, on which he built a house.[95]

Several years later, the settler's house was converted into a bed and breakfast, called the *Corbett House Bed and Breakfast*. The B&B is located on Corbett Road. Phone: (250) 629-6305

Delia'S SHaNgri-La OceaNFroNt B&B

Delia's Shangri-La Oceanfront Bed and Breakfast is a B&B on the southern shore of North Pender. It is located on Pirates Road. Phone: 1-877-629-2800

NoSey PoiNt INN

The *Nosey Point Inn* is a Victorian style house that once sat in the heart of Victoria. It is now located on Hamilton Road, on the eastern shore of North Pender. Phone: (250) 629-3617

PoetS Cove ReSort & Spa

Initially, settlers living on South Pender would row to Saturna Island for supplies.[96] In the 1930's, the first store to be constructed on South Pender was built at a harbour.[97]

PeNder Islands

Bedwell Harbour Marina, early 1900's – Pender Islands Museum

A few years later, a couple built a marina at the harbour. At the time, they were living in a building that was once a community hall. They had moved it to the harbour, and then expanded it to accommodate a cafe.[98]

In 1960, a hotel, called the *Bedwell Harbour Hotel*, was built at the harbour.[99] The hotel was later converted into a resort called the *Bedwell Harbour Resort*.[100]

A few years prior to this writing, new owners expanded and renamed the resort *Poet's Cove Resort and Spa*.

Bedwell Harbour Marina as it appears today

Today, Poet's Cove Resort is the only center on South Pender. Located on Bedwell Harbour, it offers 46 rooms, villas and cottages, and provides for an activity centre, tennis courts and a swimming pool. The *Susurrus Spa* offers six treatment rooms.

The *Bedwell Harbour Marina* at the harbour is a full-service, deep-moorage marina and boat rental.

A Canada Customs point of entry is located at the marina. It processes more than 9,000 vessels each year. Because it attracts boaters from both sides of the border, Bedwell Harbour is the busiest port on the Penders.

The resort and marina are located on Gowlland Point Road. Reservations are recommended. Phone: 1-888-512-7638

WaterFroNt WilderNeSS

Waterfront Wilderness is a cottage rental on the southeast side of North Pender. It is located on Canal Road. Phone: (250) 629-6417

SuN RaveN WelLNeSS Retreat & B&B

The *Sun Raven Wellness Retreat and B&B* is a wellness retreat on the northwest side of North Pender. Located on MacKinnon Road, it offers a pool, sauna, massage and Reiki treatments. Phone: (250) 629-6216

Ways to Get Around

During World War II, a resident purchased a boat, called the *Blue Streak*, and started a water taxi service. For many years, he made Saturday trips, carrying people to Vancouver Island to do their shopping. He operated the service for 20 years, until he sold the business in the 1960's.[101]

Today, Pender is one of the prime areas for boating in the Gulf Islands. It provides easy access to some hot kayaking spots, such as around Bedwell Harbour. Late summer and fall is the best time to kayak because of morning and evening calms. You can also travel by *stinkpot* (motorboat) or by sailboat, in Navy Channel and in Plumper Sound.

Driftwood Auto Centre

The *Driftwood Auto Centre* provides bicycles and scooters for touring around the Penders. It is located at the Driftwood Centre on Bedwell Harbour Road.

Seair Sea Planes

Seair Sea Planes offers daily, scheduled, float plane flights between Port Washington and the airport on the mainland. Phone: 1-800-44SEAIR

PeNder ISLaNds

Harbour Air

Harbour Air offers daily, scheduled, float plane flights between the mainland and Bodwell Harbour. The planes that are used for the flights are called 'Beavers'. Phone: 1-800-665-0212

Kayak PeNder ISLaNd

Kayak Pender Island is a fully licensed kayak tour business that offers tours, lessons and rentals. It is located at the Otter Bay Marina and also operates out of Poets Cove Resort.

Brackett Cove FarM

Brackett Cove Farm offers trail rides around the Penders. It is located on Razor Point Road. Phone: (250) 629-3306

PeNder ISLaNds Taxi & Tours

If you need to get somewhere quickly, and you do not have your own *island beater* (old car parked on the Penders), you can hail *Pender Islands Taxi and Tours*, a licensed, year round taxi and tour company.

Reportedly, it is the only taxi service company in all of British Columbia to use Land Rovers®. Phone (250) 629-3555.

SouNd PaSSage AdveNtures

Sound Passage Adventures offers whale watching and eco tours, as well as scuba diving, fishing charters, and kayak and paddle boat rentals. Phone: 1-877-629-3930

PacıFıc SHoreLıNe AdveNtures

Pacific Shoreline Adventures offers sightseeing and scuba diving tours. It is located on Pirates Road. Phone: (250) 629-9950

GuLF ISLaNdS Water Taxı

Operating from Salt Spring Island, *Gulf Islands Water Taxi* provides scheduled trips between Port Washington and Salt Spring Island. Phone (250) 537-2510

Razor PoıNt Boat CHarters

Razor Point Boat Charters provides for a charter fishing and sightseeing vessel, with a veteran commercial fisherman as a guide. The boat can accommodate up to four people. The charter company is located on Razor Point Road. Phone: (250) 629-9922

Pender Islands
Sights & Shops

1 The Canal &
   Helisen Archaeological Site
2 St. Peter's Anglican Church
3 The General Store
4 Old Orchard Farm
5 Church of the Good Shepherd
6 United Community Church
7 Pender Islands Cemetery
8 The Driftwood Centre
9 Hope Bay Stores
10 Pender Islands Museum
11 Pender Island Pottery
12 Renaissance Studio &
   Shepherd's Croft Farm
13 Armstrong Studio
14 Wildart Photography Studio
15 The Wool Shed
16 Mooring's Market
17 Buttonlady's Gallery
18 NatureDiver Gallery
19 Blood Star Studio & Gallery

THiNgS to See

The Pender Islands are scenic getaways with a variety of areas to explore. Many people come to Pender to partake in the events or go for a hike in the forest.

North Pender consists of four major routes. Port Washington Road runs east and west, connecting the two wharves. Bedwell Harbour Road runs north and south, bisecting the Island, and then splits off at Schooner Way, which connects several minor roads along the south end of the Island.

South Otter Bay Road turns into Otter Bay Road, which connects Bedwell Harbour Road to the ferry terminal.

South Pender, which consists of only one major route, is connected to North Pender via Canal Road. It runs east and west along the north end of the Island. Canal Road turns into Spalding Road, and then into Gowlland Point Road, which runs along the south end of the Island.

SHepHerd'S CroFt FarM

Shepherd's Croft Farm is a unique roadside stand with a number of oddities on display. It is located on Port Washington Road. (#12 on the map)

> **Treasure Hunt**
> *There is a plaque, which was dedicated to the editor of the Pender Post. Can you find it on the Penders?*

THe CaNaL

Initially, a strip of land, called *Indian Portage*, joined North and South Pender Islands. At that time, the Portage was a meeting place for settlers living on Saturna and South Pender Islands.[102] The area made history when Indians shot two settlers there in the 1860's.[103]

Whenever settlers wanted to travel between Bedwell Harbour and Browning Harbour, they would carry their boats across the Portage, in order to avoid having to make the dangerous voyage around South Pender.[104]

At the turn of the century, a petition was circulated around the Pender Islands requesting that a canal be dredged, to enable the S.S. *Iroquois* to make a speedier passage around the Islands.[105] The canal that was eventually dredged is self-scouring.

PeNder IsLaNds

The canal separating North and South Pender Islands, early 1900's - BC Archives G-06190

In 1950, residents requested that a bridge be built across the canal. However, reportedly, the Federal Government disclaimed any responsibility for the blasting that took place when the canal was dredged.[106]

Eventually, the government accepted responsibility for the work that was done[107] and a single-lane bridge was built five years later, reuniting North and South Pender.[108] A marching band entertained the many dignitaries who attended the official opening.[109]

The bridge, which linked the two Islands at the two harbours, made Vancouver Island more accessible. This caused traffic traveling between the Penders and Vancouver Island to double.[110]

In the 1970's, a monument was erected to commemorate the events that had unfolded at the site over the previous one hundred years.

Today, the canal, which is now twice its original width, can be crossed by way of the bridge on Canal Road. (#1 on the map)

The canal as it appears today

HeLiSeN ArcHeoLogicaL Site

The midden and surrounding areas of Bedwell Harbour are a burial grounds for the *Tsawout* and *Tseycum* First Nations, who lived in the area seasonally.[111] When the canal was dredged at the turn of the century, several artifacts left by the Indians were unearthed.[112]

As vessels traveled through the canal, erosion began to damage the remains of the area. As a result, it was designated a Provincial Heritage Site.[113]

Today, *Helisen Archeological Site* is one of the largest archeological excavations in all the Gulf Islands. Excavations of the site have resulted in the discovery of thousands of artifacts, some of which are on display at the Pender Islands Public Library.

A monument was recently erected at the site, commemorating the First Nations. The site can be accessed by way of Canal Road. (#1 on the map)

Hope Bay Stores

Initially, the people of North Pender ordered their provisions and other goods by mail order, which were brought by boat to one of the two wharves.[114]

When Corbett's store opened at Hope Bay at the turn of the century, it was the first store on the Penders.[115] It served local residents, as well as settlers from neighboring Saturna and Mayne Islands. It also provided a second home for the post office.[116]

The storekeeper asked all the ladies on the island to make up grocery lists indicating their favorite brands.[117] They ordered long, black-beaded hatpins for their wide-brimmed hats, high-button shoes, as well as wool cashmere and pure silk stockings. The men generally shopped for gunpowder and buckshot. The supplies were then brought in to the store by the S.S. *Iroquois*.[118]

Corbett's store became very successful, eventually expanding into hardware and farm supplies.[119] Before the onset of World War I, a new store with two small warehouses was built. A few years later, the two warehouses were replaced with a two-storey structure.[120]

In the 1920's, the store was modernized with an electric plant, refrigerator and ice cream cabinet. It was then further enlarged at the back.[121]

When the store was sold in the 1950's, it held claim to being the oldest, established, Gulf Islands general store to have operated under the same management for at least four decades.[122] On the firm's monthly accounts were many names of customers who had frequented the store when it first opened.[123]

The new owners changed the name of the store to *Smith Brothers*.[124] Later, it was shortened to *Smith's* and was then changed to the *Hope Bay Store*.[125]

In the 1960's, the Hope Bay Store ceased to operate as a grocery store and became home to various arts and crafts stores. It closed its doors in the 1980's.[126]

Hope Bay Stores in the 1970's – Hope Bay Rising Holdings Ltd.

A few years prior to this writing, the original buildings at the Hope Bay Store were razed in an early morning fire. The property was partially restored, and then purchased in a foreclosure sale by a cooperative of Islanders who completed the restoration.[127]

The new, two-storey complex, which is located at the end of Port Washington Road, houses a variety of businesses. (#9 on the map) The renovation project was recently nominated for a Commercial Building Award, which recognized it for its exceptional quality.

The original owners of the store still conduct business near the new stores, as *R.S.W. Corbett and Son.* Their company is one of the oldest firms still doing business in the Gulf Islands.[128]

Old Orchard Farm

At the turn of the century, the settler who would later operate the General Store purchased the farm from which **the Postman** had provided postal service. The settler called the farm *Sunny Side Ranch.*[129]

Over the years, the settler and his wife made many changes to the single-gable cabin on the old farm. They substantially enlarged it, and then added a veranda and bay windows to it.[130]

Although it had an abundance of exterior doors, they never removed them. As a result, it is difficult for guests to determine which door to enter through, even today.[131]

The couple created a floor-to-ceiling collage of calendars, greeting cards, magazine clippings and photographs in the hall and in the study. At one end of the living room, they used oil paints to paint a large landscape. Beneath the chair rails, at the opposite end of the room, they painted a floral scene.[132]

Eventually, the space that had been used as a mailroom by **the Postman** was converted into a dining room.[133]

Old Orchard Farm in 1925 - BC Archives C-07017

Throughout the orchard, the settler installed an elaborate irrigation system of water pipes.[134] Later, he opened a tennis court on the lawn and the first tennis club was formed there.[135] It served as the site of many inter-Island tennis matches during the 1920's.[136]

In the late 1930's, new owners covered all the walls with plywood, concealing the collages and paintings. Then, they added a second storey as an apartment, which they rented to numerous tenants through the years.[137]

Much later, in the 1970's, the property was sold again and renamed *Old Orchard Farm*. Recently, when the new owners began restoring the old home, they discovered the artwork that had been boarded up by the previous owners.[138]

Old Orchard Farm as it appears today

Today, the meticulously restored Old Orchard Farm is a private residence on Port Washington Road. (#4 on the map) The house, which is nearly five times the size of the original building, can be seen through one of the finest ancient orchards on the Penders. The orchard is still producing over 40 varieties of apples, pears and plums.[139]

UNited CoMMuNity CHurCH

In the 1890's, the work of the Presbyterian Church began on North Pender. Services were held in the community hall, and a set of used Sankey hymnbooks and an organ were donated.[140]

A missionary, who had accepted the task of pioneering the work, made the first set of slatted benches. He also built a rowboat to provide transportation to and from the services. At the turn of the century, the first ordained minister was appointed and a gas-powered boat was built for his use.[141]

That same year, a very prominent settler donated some land for a church and the *Pender Island Presbyterian Church* was soon built on a hill overlooking Hope Bay. In the 1920's, a Manse was built below the church, for use as the Reverend's residence.[142]

Four years later, the Presbyterian Church merged into the United Church of Canada and the church building became known as the *United Community Church.*[143]

United Community Church in 1946
Pender Islands Museum

In the late 1980's, when the Roman Catholics had no venue in which to hold church services on the Penders, the

United Community Church building was used as a location for Catholic services.[144]

Today, the United Community Church is the oldest church on the Penders. Located on Bedwell Harbour Road, it operates as a non-denominational church,[145] while Catholic services are now held in a house in Magic Lake Estates. (#6 on the map)

United Community Church as it appears today

PeNder ISLaNdS CeMetery

At the turn of the century, a prominent settler donated some land for the development of an Island cemetery. Maintenance of the cemetery was a community responsibility.[146]

Because there was no church on the Island at the time, funeral services were always held at one of the settlers' homes. A horse-drawn wagon would then travel to the cemetery and friends would prepare the grave.[147]

In the 1950's, wrought iron gates were donated to the cemetery. A decade later, two residents donated some land so the cemetery could be enlarged.[148]

Recently, the Pender Islands' Museum Society donated a 100-year time capsule to the cemetery. It had been started at the turn of the century by a settler who lived on Hope Bay.[149] The cemetery is located on Browning Harbour Road.[150] (#7 on the map)

St. Peter's ANgLicaN CHurcH

Before the first church was built on North Pender, **the Postman** would row to Mayne Island to attend church services. Sometimes, his own home was used as a place of worship. Later, the Port Washington Community Hall was used for holding church services. [151]

Just before the outbreak of World War I, the owner of the General Store donated some land for a church. [152] The 50-person church was called *St. Peter's Anglican Church* and **the Postman** was instrumental in the building of it. [153]

Several items were donated to the church, including an antique silver chalice, a patent from England and an Italian marble font. [154]

In the 1920's, a cottage was built behind the church so the visiting clergy had a place in which to live during their visits. It was later renovated to provide a vestry for a resident Vicar. [155]

During the 1940's, a Reverend served both St. Peter's Church and a church on South Pender. When his successor drowned in a storm shortly after starting parish work, a carved Oak lectern and a prayer desk were placed in the church, as memorials to both Reverends. [156]

Originally, St. Peter's Anglican Church was located at Port Washington. However, a decade ago, it was moved to a more central location on Canal Road, where it now sits beside a hall, [157] called *Parish Hall*. (#2 on the map)

PeNder ISLaNdS MuSeuM

At the turn of the century, a Scottish family purchased some land on a bay, where they established a farm. [158]

Soon, they built a cabin for their friends to vacation in. Their friends enjoyed it so much that the family decided to develop the property into a resort. They called it *Roesland Resort*. [159]

Each winter, they added more cabins to the resort. Because the cabins only included the basic of necessities, their guests brought their own bedding and dishes, and carried their own water.[160]

By the 1920's, a son had taken over the resort. He built a general store on the property, for the use of his guests. He also maintained a gas station on nearby Roe Islet.[161]

By the 1950's, there were 17 cabins at Roesland Resort, each with its own bed, kitchen and outhouse. For those who could secure a reservation, it was one of the most popular vacation destinations in the southern Gulf Islands. The property was sold to new owners in the 1970's, who continued to run it as a resort, but built their own home on the property.[162]

In the 1990's, the resort was closed, after operating for over 70 years. Many of the regulars had been third and fourth generation guests.[163] When the land was purchased for use as a park, the owners were granted a life-long tenancy on the property.[164]

Recently, the Pender Islands Museum Society restored the family's house, and then converted it into an historical museum.[165] In the year prior to this writing, the *Pender Islands Museum* opened on South Otter Bay Road. (#10 on the map)

CHUɼCH oF tHe Good SHepHeɼd

In the 1930's, a Reverend gave the fittings from a log chapel on Saturna

Island to be used in the construction of a church on South Pender. An English woman who owned the land on which the church was built donated a substantial amount of money to its construction.[166]

Church of the Good Shepherd, early 1900's - Pender Islands Museum

The following year, the *Church of The Good Shepherd* was opened. Several items were donated to the church, including the altar and altar cloth, some furniture, the tower bell, the baptismal font and a stained glass window.[167]

To commemorate the coronation of King George VI, an Oak tree was planted on the church grounds. At the front of the grounds was erected a *lych* gate, in memory of an early settler and his wife.[168]

**Church of the Good Shepherd
as it appears today**

Today, the lych gate provides for a traditional English entrance to the church, which is located on Gowlland Point Road. (#5 on the map)

The GeNeraL Store

When the General Store opened at Port Washington, it became the social center for the community and also the home of the post office. The builder of the store was its first proprietor. Reportedly, he had no experience as a storekeeper, but because he was a generous man, the store thrived.[169]

One day, an evaporated milk salesman offered the storekeeper a discount on case lots. Although he had little hope of selling them, the storekeeper ordered 50 cases. For a while thereafter, every time an Indian would arrive at Port Washington from Galiano Island, he would leave with a can of milk.[170]

Over the years, the store changed owners several times. Between the 1940's and 60's, a very small library operated from the store.[171]

The General Store in 1947 - BC Archives I-20737

When the store changed hands in the 1970's, the new owners ran it primarily as a grocery store.[172]

The General Store in the 1970's
Pender Islands Museum

A decade after the post office was re-located, the store closed, having been continuously operated as a grocery store for over 75 years.[173] It then operated for several more years as a retail outlet for local artists.[174]

The General Store as it appears today

In the year prior to this writing, the community put it in Trust, using the strongest legal protection that exists for a heritage building. Then, they began to restore it. The store is located at the end of Bridges Road. (#3 on the map)

PLaceS to Eat

In the 1890's, a settler and his family purchased some land at the harbour on North Pender. The settler's wife hung a gong in the front yard, from chains that were fastened between two Fir trees. She would strike it with a sledge, creating a sound that could be heard for miles.[175]

For many years, the other settlers had their lives guided by the woman's gong, which they called 'Brackett's Bell'. Every day, at noon, she used Brackett's Bell to inform the working men that it was time for lunch. She used different signals for calling individual family members and for calling the family of a stonecutter who lived across the bay.[176]

Today, whatever you hunger or thirst for, there are a variety of good restaurants on the Pender Islands where you can get great *muckamuck* (food) and drink.

CHIppers CaFé

Chipper's Café is located on North Pender, at the Pender Island Golf and Country Club. It provides for casual dining and beverage service. They also cater golf tournaments and private functions. Phone: (250) 629-6665

PIStoU GRILL CasUaL BIStRo

The *Pistou Grill Casual Biotro* is located on North Pender, at the Driftwood Centre. It offers lunch and dinner. Dinner reservations are recommended. Phone: (250) 629-3131

Hope Bay CaFé

The *Hope Bay Café* is open for breakfast, lunch and dinner. It is located on North Pender, at the Hope Bay Stores.

PeNdeR ISLaNd BaKeRy

The *Pender Island Bakery* is located on North Pender, at the Driftwood Center. It provides for coffee, soups, sandwiches and baked goods.

THe ISLaNdeRS ReStaURaNt

The Islanders Restaurant offers a fine dining menu of steak, chicken, pasta and seafood. It is located on North Pender, on MacKinnon Road. Reservations are recommended. Phone: (250) 629-3929.

That Little Coffee Place

That Little Coffee Place serves coffee and pastries. Formerly, a gift shop, the coffee shop is located on Schooner Way in Magic Lake Estates.

Memories at The Inn

Memories At The Inn is a restaurant located on North Pender, on Canal Road. They offer chicken, seafood, ribs and pasta. If you have a craving for pizza, you can get it there. Phone: 1-800-550-0172

Sh-Qu-Ala Inn

The *Sh-Qu-Ala Inn* is a licensed pub located at the Port Browning Marina Resort on North Pender. Phone: (250) 629-3493

Aurora Restaurant & Lounge

The *Aurora Restaurant* is located on South Pender, at the Poets Cove Resort. They serve breakfast, lunch and dinner, featuring local, West Coast cuisine. Phone: 1-888-512-7638

Port Browning Café

The *Port Browning Café* offers breakfast, lunch and dinner. It is located on North Pender, at the Port Browning Marina Resort. Phone: (250) 629-3493

PLaceS to SHoP

In the 1960's, a group of artists on the Pender Islands began gathering together to sketch and paint. Soon, they were organizing workshops at the Royal Canadian Legion hall and exhibitions at the Port Washington hall. For a while, they made their home in the old school at Hope Bay.[177]

| **Treasure Hunt** |
| *A small railway crossing sits on a residential property. Can you find it on the Penders?* |

One of the first art shows held by the group was at the Legion hall. Another show was held at the golf course. The fourth show was held in the 1970's, at the old community hall.[178]

Today, there are several art galleries, shops and studios situated along Port Washington Road. Known locally as *Gallery Row*, the stretch of roadway provides visitors to the Penders the opportunity to pick up a *potlatch* (gift) for someone special. Watch for road signs and the chance to meet an artist working in their studio.

Recently, the Pender Islands Artisan Cooperative opened a gallery to make it possible for the variety of fine artisans on the Penders to display their works. Located at the Hope Bay Stores on Port Washington Road, the gallery is called the *Red Tree Gallery*.

Gwen's Fine Art

Gwen's Fine Art is located on North Pender, at the Driftwood Centre. It offers fine native art and gifts. (#8 on the map)

Sladen's Gift Shop

Sladen's Gift Shop is located on North Pender, at the Hope Bay Stores. It offers fine home decor. (#9 on the map)

Casual Pender - Unique Gifts

Casual Pender – Unique Gifts provides for an enticing variety of gifts, clothing and jewelry. It is located on North Pender, at the Driftwood Centre. (#8 on the map)

Talisman Books & Gallery Ltd.

Talisman Books and Gallery is a fine bookstore gallery, which offers a wide selection of new and used books, as well as quality glass and pottery created by local artisans. It is located on North Pender, at the Driftwood Centre. (#8 on the map)

Pender Island Pottery

In the 1890's, a very prominent settler emigrated from Scotland to North Pender with his family.[179] Eventually, he and his son built a home on their farm.[180]

The settler and his son also built tennis courts on their farm. The first tennis matches played on the Penders were reported to have been held there.[181]

In the 1920's, the farm was passed down to the settler's grandson, who raised sheep, and Jersey and Angus cattle there. The farm remained in the family for many decades.[182]

Home to *Pender Island Pottery*, the settler's house is the oldest farmhouse on the Penders today.[183] The new owners use the house as their workshop. It is located on North Pender, on Port Washington Road. (#11 on the map)

The GoldsMith

The Goldsmith is a jewelry store that specializes in custom goldsmithing, diamonds, gemstones, knives and repairs. It is located on North Pender, at the Hope Bay Stores. (#9 on the map)

ReNaissaNce Studio

The *Renaissance Studio* is an art gallery that offers art and antiques, as well as renowned custom, hand-made jewelry. It is located on North Pender, on Port Washington Road. (#12 on the map)

PeNder IsLaNds

The Wool Shed

In the 1920's, a settler bought a small house on a bay. To supplement his income, he and his family built three cottages on the property and opened his house to guests.[184]

The family called their resort the *Welcome Bay Inn.* They supplied their guests with home-cooked meals, which they served in their dining room.[185]

The resort closed at the onset of World War II,[186] after which the Royal Canadian Legion used one of the guest cottages as their meeting place for a while.[187]

Today, the property is called *Welcome Bay Farm* and a descendant of the settler still resides there.

The owners of the farm raise goats and sheep on the property. They also run a studio called *The Wool Shed,* in which they shear, spin and hand-dye wool.[188]

The farm and studio are located on North Pender, on Clam Bay Road. (#15 on the map)

PeNder TreaSureS CoNSigNMeNt & GiFt

Pender Treasures Consignment and Gift is located on North Pender, at the Hope Bay Stores. It offers local crafts, body care, clothing, books and gifts. (#9 on the map)

Mooring's Market

Mooring's Market is located on South Pender, at Poet's Cove Resort. (#16 on the map) It provides for gifts, as well as specialty coffees, ice cream and sandwiches.

NatureDiver GaLLery

The *NatureDiver Gallery* offers photographs of wildlife, including underwater scenes. It is located on South Pender, on Boundary Pass Drive. (#18 on the map)

Armstrong Studio

The *Armstrong Studio* provides for oil and watercolor paintings. It is located on North Pender, on Otter Bay Road. (#13 on the map)

Benevolent Beast Studio Gallery

The *Benevolent Beast Studio* offers paintings, mixed media and sculpture. It is located on North Pender, on Bedwell Harbour Road. (#14 on the map)

Blood Star Studio & Gallery

The *Blood Star Studio and Gallery* provides for drawings and folk art. It is located on South Pender, on Jennens Road. (#19 on the map)

Wildart Photography Gallery

The *Wildart Photography Gallery* offers a selection of over 8,000 images, specializing in hard-to-access wilderness areas of British Columbia. The gallery is located on North Pender, on Bedwell Harbour Road. (#14 on the map)

Buttonlady's Gallery

The *Buttonlady's Gallery* offers handmade ceramic buttons, embellishments and original art. It is located on Frigate Road in Magic Lake Estates. (#17 on the map)

Events to Attend

Before the turn of the century, evening entertainment on the Pender Islands was organized in a local hall or school. Later, an organist formed the Pender Island Choral Society, which put on some outstanding concerts.[189]

Each summer, one or two public picnics were held, usually on Victoria Day or on Dominion Day. At the picnics, races were run, sports were played and good food was eaten.[190]

Whether it is an annual event, such as the *Garden Party* or the *Fall Fair*, or a special event, such as a music festival or play, there is always something to take in on the Penders today.

Pender Islands' Soccer Team in 1932 - Salt Spring Archives 56

PeNder IsLaNds

The Pender Island Lions Club has been active for over 30 years[191] and a few years prior to this writing, the Pender Island Volunteer Firefighter's Association was formed.[192] Both organizations host a variety of events throughout the year.

Easter CeLebratIoNs

The annual *Easter Egg Hunt* is an event that is held every Easter at the Port Browning Marina. Children scatter across the field in search of hundreds of tiny chocolate Easter Eggs hidden in the rocks and grass.

The *South Pender Easter Art Walk* is an annual event that has been taking place at Easter since the late 1990's. Look for the yellow balloons to guide you around the studios and galleries on South Pender.

PeNder IsLaNd HeaLtH & WeLLNeSS FaIr

The *Wellness Fair* is an annual event that takes place in May, at the Pender Island Community Hall. It provides for therapies and products for creating a healthy mind, body and spirit. Demonstrations include Tai Chi, Qi Gong and crystal bowls. There are also door prizes.

PeNder IsLaNds FarMer'S MarKet

The *Pender Island Farmer's Market*, which runs every Saturday from May to October, is held at both the Pender Islands Community Hall and the Driftwood Centre. The market provides for a cornucopia of fresh produce from local farmers, as well as art from local artists and craftspeople.

PeNder INvItatIoNaL DIsc TourNaMeNt

On the last weekend in May, the annual *Pender Island Invitational Disc*

Tournament attracts almost 100 participants of frisbee golf from all over the West Coast. The tournament takes place at the Golf Island Disc Park. Use of the course is free, but players are required to bring their own frisbees.

CaNada Day CeLebratioN

Canada Day Celebrations are held each year on July 1, at the Pender Islands Community Hall. There is food, events and a variety of festivities.

Art OFF THe FeNce SHoW

Art Off The Fence is an outdoor art show and sale that has been taking place since the 1990's. The event is held in July, on South Pender Island.

PeNder ISLaNdS Art SHoW

The *Pender Islands Art Show* is an annual event, which has been taking place since the 1970's. Today, there are over 30 artists displaying drawings, fabric art and collages, as well as watercolors, oils and acrylics.

GardeN Party

St. Peter's Guild grew out of a Women's Auxiliary, which included many pioneer women from Port Washington.[193]

In the early 1930's, they started hosting a fair to raise funds for the Columbia Coast Mission, the Salvation Army and other causes.[194] Reportedly, the fair was always held at a private residence, in their garden. Thereafter, it became known as the *Garden Party*.

Today, the Garden Party provides for games and prizes, as well as a flea market. It is held each year in July, at the Parish Hall beside St. Peter's Anglican Church.

PeNdeR ISLaNdS

Yacht Club Regatta

The annual *Yacht Club Regatta* takes place in *Navy Channel* and *Plumper Sound*, the waters bounded by Mayne, Saturna and the Pender Islands. During the event, an estimated 600 sailors occupy Port Browning Marina for a full week in August.

Officially known as *RIPS Canadian Race Week*, the regatta is fashioned after the highly successful Whidbey Island Race Week and is open to all types of sailboats. The event includes daily racing and prizes, as well as barbecues, beer gardens, a dance and other activities.

PeNdeR ISLaNdS FaLL FaiR

The first *Pender Islands Fall Fair* was held during the depression of the 1930's, at the Hope Bay Community Hall. In an effort to encourage them to plant vegetables to enter in the fair, the Farmers' Institute gave seeds to all the children living on the Island. Then, they came to the children's homes to inspect their gardens.[195]

Initially, the sponsoring community groups had to borrow folding tables for the fair and haul them across the Island for each and every event, including the evening dance, which was a highlight.[196]

In the first year of the fair, a settler's son won first prize for his entry. He took a vacation with his winnings.[197]

Another year, a woman decided to enter a cake decorated like the Union Jack, which was the national flag at the time. When she discovered that she had run out of blue food coloring, she used ink, instead. The cake won first prize.[198]

The fall fair was terminated at the onset of World War II and was not re-introduced until the 1960's.[199]

Today, the Pender Islands Fall Fair takes place in August, at the Pender Islands Community Hall. There are 1,000 exhibits entered each year, in a variety of categories. Judging takes place in numerous events and the fair is still followed by a dance.

HaLLoWeeN HoWL

The *Halloween Howl* is held at the Pender Islands Community Hall. It provides for a dance, games and prizes for the best costume. There is also a fireworks display.

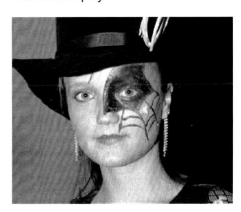

CHrıStMaS CeLeLratıoNS

In the 1940's, a prominent Englishman moved to the Penders from the mainland.[200] In the year 1960, he and his wife decided to solicit donations for CARE Canada. For every donation, he placed a Christmas light on a tall Fir tree that was growing in their garden. He called it *The Tree of Light*.[201]

The first year, the couple raised just over one hundred dollars from donations. Each year, the amount grew higher until, by the 1970's, they had raised thousands of dollars for CARE Canada.[202]

Eventually, the Pender Island Lions Club took over the project from the man, who was 89 years old at the time. By the 1990's, it was estimated that

The Lions club had donated over $140,000.[203]

The Tree of Light, which is now known as the CARE Tree, has been moved more than once since the inception of the project.[204]   Today, it shines on Bridges Road.

The Bellingham Central Lions Club, in Washington State, continue the Christmas season by loading a *Christmas Ship* with toys and gifts, and sending it to the Penders.

Known locally as the *Santa Ship*, the Christmas Ship is greeted at the Port Washington wharf, and then Santa and his 'helpers' distribute gifts to the kids.

Residents of the Penders also celebrate the Christmas season with a craft fair held at the Pender Islands Community Hall.   The fair includes a silent auction and raffle.

The season is completed with carols sung by the Otter Bay Symphony Orchestra and Choral Society. The event takes place on Christmas Eve at Hyashi Cove.

NeW Year'S CeLebratioNS

The *Magic Lake Lantern Festival* is a theatrical production that is held on New Year's Eve at Magic Lake, in Magic Lake Estates. It is put on by the Three On The Tree theatre production company.

Spectators carry lit sparklers around the lake during the events, which include fire spinners, stilt walkers and a lantern ballet on the lake.

The lantern festival is followed by a *Masquerade Ball*, which is held at the Pender Islands Community Hall. Live entertainment is provided.

On New Year's Day, residents of the Penders choose between golfing in the *New Year's Golf Tournament* and swimming at the annual *Polar Bear Swim* at Hamilton Beach. Spectators are welcome.

Pender Islands
Parks & Beaches

1 Susan Point	2 Davidson Bay
3 Bricky Bay	4 Welcome Bay
5 Mt. Elizabeth Pk	6 George Hill Pk
7 Grimmer Bay	8 James Point
9 Hyashi Cove	10 Irene Bay
11 Roesland Pk & Roe Lk	12 Shingle Bay Pk
13 Panda Bay	14 Thieves Bay Pk
15 Boat Nook	16 Prior Centennial Pk
17 Oak Bluffs	18 Wallace Point
19 Medicine Beach	20 Danny Martin Pk
22 Mt. Menzies Pk	23 Mt Norman Regional Pk
	24 Cedar Creek
	25 Little Bay
	26 Teece Point
	27 Gowlland Point
	28 Drummond Bay
	29 Beaumont Marine Pk
	30 Enchanted Forest
	31 Abbott Hill Pk & Magic Lk
	32 Lilias Spalding Pk
	33 Mortimer Spit Pk
	34 Fawn Creek Pk
	35 Lively Peak Pk
	36 Hope Bay
	37 Hamilton Beach

Parks to Visit

In the year prior to this writing, a small, single-engine plane crashed on protected land on the Pender Islands. The pilot, who was flying with his five-year old son, managed to call 911 from his cellular phone. Emergency personnel traveled through dense forest and steep terrain to reach them.[205]

A portion of the land on the Penders is protected within the Gulf Islands National Park Reserve. In addition, there are numerous smaller parks outside the reserve.

The trails range from seashore-access, walking trails to forest hikes, so you might want to invest in a pair of *waffle stompers* (hiking shoes). As well as ensuring that nothing is left on the trails, hikers should take as much of their *iktas* (belongings) as possible off the Island.

Abbott Hill Park

In the 1960's, daily ferry service from Vancouver Island brought land speculators to the Penders.[206]

When it was completed in the 1970's, *Magic Lake Estates*, on the west side of North Pender, was the largest planned subdivision in all of Canada. Originally called *Gulf Garden Estates*, it was heavily marketed in the cities.[207] Soon, most of the lots were sold[208] and newcomers began to build summer cabins and retirement homes there.

Abbott Hill Park is named after the surveyor who purchased the land that is now the Magic Lake Estates development.[209]

The steep trail through the park is accessible by way of Spyglass Road, in Magic Lake Estates. (#31 on the map)

Danny Martin Park

Danny Martin Park is located on the west side of North Pender, in Magic Lake Estates. It is a recreational park that provides for a playground and baseball diamond. There are also facilities for picnics if you want to stay awhile. The park is accessible by way of Schooner Way. (#20 on the map)

The easy, 2 km interpretive trail winds through the park and leads to a seasonal waterfall. It can be accessed at the end of Spalding Road. (#30 on the map)

Enchanted Forest Park

The *Enchanted Forest Park* is a beautiful wetland on the west side of South Pender.

Fawn Creek Park

Fawn Creek Park is set in a mature forest of large, spectacular Western Red Cedar and Douglas-Fir, on the northwest tip of South Pender.

PeNdeR ISLaNdS

Fawn Creek is a seasonal creek that flows through the park and into the ocean. The trail through the park is accessible by way of steps off Ainslie Point Road. (#34 on the map)

George HiLL ParK

George Hill Park, on the northern tip of North Pender, provides for a forest hike to two viewpoints. The challenging, 2 km trail is accessible from the corner of Walden Road and Ogden Road. (#6 on the map)

LiLiaS SpaLdiNg HeRitage ParK

In the 1880's, an Englishman purchased some land in what is now known as the *Spalding Valley*. There, he established a farm and became the very first permanent settler on South Pender.[210]

Initially, the settler lived in a log cabin, which he built on a site now known as *Ingos Corner*. In the late 1880's, he hired a builder to construct a three-bedroom frame home with three fireplaces. The house also had a large verandah, which overlooked his farm. That same year, he brought his new wife to live in his home.[211]

His wife was a good shot and would shoot at the deer if they ate the crops.[212] She baked bread, and made butter, cottage cheese and preserves. When the grapes were ripe, she made wine.

Whenever a pig was slaughtered, the woman rendered the lard, and cured hams and bacon.[213]

The settler owned a library of 2,000 books. While he read, wrote poetry and sketched,[214] his wife spun wool, which she then dyed[215] by hand.

Home of the South Pender Postmistress in 1908 – David Spalding

At the turn of the century, a wharf was built in Bedwell Harbour. When the S.S. *Iroquois* began sailing through the Gulf Islands, the delivery of mail began once a week to the new wharf.[216]

At that time, the settler's wife became the Postmistress for South Pender, sorting the mail at the end of the wharf.[217]

Shortly thereafter, the crew of the HMS *Egeria* landed on the bay to study the tides. To carry out their duties, they built a small hut at the head of the wharf. When the crew departed three years later, the couple fell heir to the little building and converted it into the *South Pender Post Office.*[218]

The delivery of mail to the post office developed into a weekly social event. The Postmistress would drive her horse and buggy from the farm to the post office, along a dangerous wagon road.[219]

If the mail was late, the woman would often wait until after midnight for it to arrive. When the residents of South Pender turned up to discuss current events, she would serve them tea and cake.[220]

In the 1930's, the little hut from which she performed her postal duties was removed from the wharf. Although her farm was sold a few years later, she continued to hold the position of Postmistress for South Pender until her death in the 1950's.[221]

Lilias Spalding Heritage Park was named after this pioneer woman, whose weaving loom can still be seen today, at the Pender Islands Museum.

The old farm is known locally as 'The Ranch'. A short trail through Lilias Spalding Park leads to the remains of one of the buildings on The Ranch.

The ruts, which are reported to have been left in the field by the settler's wagon, can still be seen there. The trail through the park is accessible from Castle Road. (#32 on the map)

There is a steeper trail to the park, which is accessible from up the road. It leads to *Spalding Hill*, which provides for great views and beautiful rock faces, and is one of the best places in the Gulf Islands to see Turkey Vultures and Bald Eagles.

Lively Peak Park

Lively Peak Park is located in the center of North Pender, in Magic Lake Estates. The park is accessible by way of a rough, steep trail off Ketch Road, which leads to a viewpoint. (#35 on the map)

MortiMer Spit park

Mortimer Spit Park is located beside the canal, on the northeastern tip of South Pender. It provides for views of Shark Cove. The park is accessible by way of Canal Road. (#33 on the map)

> **Treasure Hunt**
> *There is a house shaped like a dome. Can you find it in Magic Lake Estates?*

MoUNt MeNzieS park

In the 1890's, **the Postman** ran an ad for a farm hand to help him farm his land in the valley.[222] The settler who filled the position worked on the farm for three years.[223] Later, he leased and then purchased his own farm, in a valley.[224]

The settler bred award-winning poultry on his farm, which he initially called the *Nob Hill Poultry Farm*, but later renamed the *Valley Home Farm*.[225] Later, when he won second prize for his Ayrshire bull at the Victoria Fair, the showing of cattle from around the Penders began.[226]

The settler entered animals at all the major fairs in the provinces. All of his cattle were on the Record of Performance Test. The first few cows of that breed ever to pass the test in Canada were from his herd.[227]

Soon, the settler purchased two Jersey cows and a bull, establishing a fine Jersey herd that also won numerous prizes. One year, he won first prize for the most milk and butterfat produced by a single cow in two days.[228]

Mount Menzies was named after this settler, who lived on his farm for over 70 years.[229] Originally named *Bald Cone*, it is a 120 m peak on the east side of North Pender, which provides for great views of Mayne and Saturna Islands.[230]

two days. He later purchased the property.[231]

Beaumont Provincial Marine Park was named after this Captain, who donated a portion of the land for its use.[232] Established in the 1960's, it is one of the most popular marine parks in the outer Gulf Islands and is one of the best places to see Garry Oak trees.

You can access the park by boat or by way of a steep trail accessible from the summit of Mount Norman, on the west side of South Pender. (#29 on the map)

The peak sits in *Mount Menzies Park*, which is part of the Gulf Islands National Park Reserve. The park provides for 2 km of moderately difficult trails through beautiful, dense Western Red Cedar and Douglas-Fir. (#22 on the map)

MouNt NormaN RegioNaL parK & BeauMoNt ProviNciaL MariNe ParK

At the turn of the century, a settler wanted to transport a log house from Saturna Island to South Pender. So he arranged with a Captain to dismantle it, transport it, and then reassemble it. The Captain completed the task in less than

Mount Norman Regional Park is connected to Beaumont Marine Park. Acquired in the 1980's, it was the first regional park established in all the Gulf Islands.

The moderately difficult trail through Mount Norman Park can be accessed from Ainslie Point Road. A longer, but more beautiful, trail can be accessed from Canal Road. (#23 on the map) The trails provide for one of the most beautiful hikes in all the Gulf Islands and lead through second-growth forest to the top of *Mount Norman*.

At 260 m, Mount Norman is the highest peak on the Penders and provides for incredible views of Vancouver Island and the San Juan Islands.[233]

OaKS BLUFF

Around the turn of the century, a Scottish stonecutter and his neighbor built a large fence on North Pender. The fence enclosed a bluff, which was then used for raising sheep.[234]

Several times a year, the men would hold a sheep run, herding the sheep from the bluff to the end of the point.

The women and children would row to the end of the point to prepare a picnic lunch for when the men arrived.[235]

Oaks Bluff, at the south end of North Pender, overlooks Swanson Channel. Known locally as *The Oaks*,[236] it is accessible by way of a steep trail on Pirates Road. The trail provides for spectacular panoramic views of Bedwell Harbour and Swanson Channel. (#17 on the map)

PeNdeR ISLaNdS

PriOr CeNteNNiaL PrOViNCiaL PaRk

Set in the shade of a dense forest, *Prior Centennial Provincial Park* is located on the south end of North Pender. It is part of the Gulf Islands National Park Reserve.

There is a steep, 1 km trail in Prior Centennial Park, called *Heart Trail*. Heart Trail connects to a network of other trails and is accessible by way of Ketch Road, in Magic Lake Estates. (#16 on the map)

RoeSLaNd PaRk

Roesland Park is dense with Western Red Cedar and Douglas-Fir, and contains a highly sensitive ecosystem. It was named after the family who developed the Roesland Resort at the turn of the century.

Established in the 1990's, Roesland Park, which is located on the west side of North Pender, is now protected as part of the Gulf Islands National Park Reserve. The family was granted a life-long tenancy on the property.[237]

The easy, 600 m trail through the park leads to a footbridge that extends to *Roe Islet*. The islet is a good place to see Arbutus trees. The trail is accessible by way of South Otter Bay Road. (#11 on the map)

ShiNgLe Bay Park

Shingle Bay Park is located on the west side of North Pender, in Magic Lake Estates. The park can be accessed from Galleon Way, or by way of trails on Masthead Crescent and Yardarm Road. (#12 on the map) There are playgrounds and facilities for picnics if you want to stay awhile.

ThieveS Bay Park

Thieves Bay Park is a recreational park on the west side of North Pender, in Magic Lake Estates. There are playgrounds and facilities for picnics if you want to stay awhile. It is accessible by way of two trails off Anchor Way. (#14 on the map)

BeacHeS to EXpLore

In the 18th century, a Spanish mariner named North and South Pender Islands, *Sayas* and *San Eusbio*.[238]

One hundred years later, the English commissioned the ship, HMS *Plumper*, to survey the waters around the southern Gulf Islands. The ship's Second Master renamed the Pender Islands after the Captain of the ship.[239]

Ironically, several years later, a descendant of this Captain was washed ashore on South Pender during a storm one Christmas Eve.[240]

Today, the Pender Islands are well known for their numerous bays and coves, which are ideal for boat moorage. The protected bays and shallow waters make it easy to find a cove to anchor in for the *poolakle* (night).

Bedwell Harbour

In the late 1700's, a Spaniard named the harbour at the head of South Pender, *Harbour of San Antonio*.[241] It was later renamed *Bedwell Harbour*.

Located on the southwest side of South Pender, Bedwell Harbour contains shell midden from a Coast Salish Indian *rancherie* (village). The beach is located in Beaumont Marine Park. You can reach it by boat or by way of a steep trail accessible from the summit of Mount Norman. (#29 on the map)

Boat Nook

Boat Nook is located on the west side of North Pender, in Magic Lake Estates. The beach is accessible by way of steps off Schooner Way. (#15 on the map)

Bricky Bay

Shortly before the outbreak of World War I, the Coast Shale Company purchased some land on a bay. There, they constructed a brick factory with grinders, mixers and ovens. Then, they laid narrow track rails that led through a tunnel to a shale pit.[242]

Before it shut down and was demolished in the 1920's, the plant, which employed about 75 men, was producing up to 300,000 bricks every day. The bricks were then shipped from a wharf in the bay.[243]

Originally named *Colston Cove*,[244] Bricky Bay is located on the northeast side of North Pender. The sandy beach at the bay is strewn with bricks that are the remains of the brickworks.

The beach is accessible by way of steps at the end of Armadale Road. There are two other beach accesses along the road, as well, just north of the bay. (#3 on the map)

CaNNed Cod Bay

At the turn of the century, a settler owned a farm on a bay. He called his farm *Southlands*.[245]

The settler made periodic trips to the U.S. to smuggle back cases of canned goods. The police had been suspicious of the smuggler for a while, but could not catch him.[246]

One day, he arrived home with a load of cans. He carried them from his boat and hid them in some thick Alder trees. Then, he began falling the Alder trees over the cans to hide them.[247]

As he was falling the trees, the police arrived to search his property for smuggled cans. As they searched, he continued falling trees. They searched everywhere, except under the falling trees and, as a result, he was never caught.[248]

Canned Cod Bay is located on the southern tip of South Pender. It provides for great views of the San Juan Islands, the Strait of Juan de Fuca and Mount Baker, in Washington State. It is also a great place to spot whales.

The beautiful pebbled beach at the bay is lined with driftwood. (#27 on the map) At low tide, you can explore shallow caverns that have been carved out by the tides. The beach is accessible by way of Gowlland Point Road.

Cedar Creek

Shortly after the turn of the century, two brothers emigrated from England and became apprentice farmers in the Spalding Valley.[249] The following year, they purchased some property from the settler who owned The Ranch on South Pender. They called the property *Cedar Creek.*[250]

Soon, the brothers constructed a cabin on their property.[251] It had a fireplace and chimney, which they built out of granite that had been hauled over from Saturna Island.[252]

When one of the brothers was killed in action in World War I, the property was passed to the surviving brother's son.[253]

The cabin, which can be seen from Canal Road, is reported to be the oldest log cabin still in use on the Penders today.[254] A descendent still owns the property.

Cedar Creek is located on the south end of South Pender. It provides for a sandy beach that is accessible by way of steps off William Walker Road. (#24 on the map)

DavidSoN Bay

In the 1890's, **the Postman** sold some of his land on a bay to a Scottish settler[255] who was known for his rowing ability.[256]

When he needed lumber to build his home, the Scotsman rowed to Vancouver Island with his sons. Then, they walked the 18 miles to Victoria to purchase it and towed it back to their property on a homemade raft.[257]

Davidson Bay was named after this settler,[258] but is known locally as *Clam Bay*. The pebbled beach at the bay is accessible by way of a stunning 1.5 km trail of moderate difficulty.

The trail to the beach at Davidson Bay is called the *Found Road Trail*. It leads through lush forest of dense Douglas-Fir and Western Red Cedar, and passes through five ecological zones. The trail is accessible by way of Clam Bay Road. (#2 on the map)

DruMMONd Bay

Drummond Bay is located on the southern tip of South Pender. At low tide, you can walk along the beach looking at the Sea Stars. There are also good views of Mount Baker in Washington State.

There are two beach accesses on Drummond Bay. (#28 on the map) A small, rocky beach, which surrounds some reefs, is accessible at low tide by way of Higgs Road.

The other access is by way of steps at the end of Craddock Road, which lead to a pebbled beach off Tilly Point. Originally named Bilk Point, Tilly Point is known for its eerie, underwater caverns, which are covered with anemones. They provide for great scuba diving at a depth of up to 9 m.

GriMMer Bay

In the 1880's, the settler who would later become **the Postman** settled in what is now called the *Grimmer Valley*. There, he built a four-room farmhouse.[259]

Because he found entering the bay near his home dangerous, the settler sometimes left his rowboat on a nearby island and swam to shore, instead.[260] Walking up from the beach was also difficult. By the time he found the trail that led to his home, he had often used up a box of matches to light his way.[261]

Nevertheless, he soon brought his young bride to live in his home. Their oldest child was the first white child born on the Penders. When his wife went into labor with their second child, they launched a boat to see a midwife on Mayne Island. However, before they reached their destination, she delivered their baby in the boat.[262]

In the early 1890's, **the Postman** built a small cabin,[263] only to sell it a few years later and move deeper into the valley. There, he developed a dairy farm. When his sons started entering his Jersey cows in all the major fairs in the province, his cattle became famous all over British Columbia.[264]

Shortly before the outbreak of World War I, he divided his farm among his children. Then, he enlarged his home and turned it into a guesthouse.[265]

Grimmer Bay, early 1900's – Pender Islands Museum

Grimmer Bay was named after **the Postman**, whose 1920's retirement home still stands overlooking the bay.

Grimmer Bay is located on the northwest side of North Pender. The sandy beach at the bay is accessible from Bridges Road. (#7 on the map)

Grimmer Bay as it appears today

If you launch a boat from the Port Washington wharf, which extends into the bay, you can travel south to Mouat Point. The shoreline between Mouat Point and Stanley Point is quite captivating.

From there, you can continue all the way to Wallace Point. However, keep in

mind that Swanson Channel can be dangerous and there are only a few places to pull out around Oaks Bluff.

HaMiLtoN BeacH

In the 1880's, a Scottish stonecutter was carving gravestones on Vancouver Island for the Mortimer Monumental Works Company. At that time, the company was also quarrying at the harbour on North Pender. Because they liked his work, they sent the settler to the harbour to help with the quarrying.[266]

Soon, the stonecutter purchased some land at the head of the harbour. There, he built a log cabin where he and his family vacationed.[267]

Three years later, his younger brother emigrated from Scotland and moved into a small frame house on the stonecutter's property.[268] At the turn of the century, when the stonecutter brought his family to live in the house full-time, his younger brother built another home nearby.[269]

Whenever there was mail to be picked up at the South Pender Post Office, one of the brothers would raise a flag on his property. Some of the other settlers would walk a long way just to see if the flag had been raised. If it had, they would then walk the rest of the way through the bush to pick up their mail.[270]

Hamilton Beach in the 1920's - Pender Islands Museum

Hamilton Beach, at the head of Browning Harbour, is named after these two brothers who, in the year 1890, also brought the first horse to the Penders.[271]

The beach, which is accessible by way of Hamilton Road, is a good place for a *soak* (swim) and provides for a wharf that is accessible off Razor Point Road. (#37 on the map)

The Port Browning Marina at the harbour offers temporary boat anchorage and there are facilities for picnics if you and your boat want to stay awhile.

If you launch a boat from the beach, you can travel south to Mortimer Spit. At certain times, you can pass through the canal and on to Peter Cove. However, because the canal is only 12 m wide and tides run up to 4 knots, it should only be navigated at slack water.

Alternatively, you can travel south to Razor Point, and then head north to Bricky Bay. However, keep in mind that tides there run up to 3 knots.

Hope Bay

In the 1870's, two settlers purchased the entire northern half of North Pender, and then built a cattle fence that spanned the width of the Island.[272]

On his portion of the land, one of the settlers built one of the first homes on the Penders. Unfortunately, a wounded buck killed him, while he was on a hunting trip. Subsequently, his brother inherited the property and lived in the home until the 1890's.[273]

The home was a little log cabin with a window on each side. The walls were built out of round Fir logs and the roof was made of split Cedar shakes.[274] The ceiling was so low that visitors had to lower their heads to move around.[275]

There was a stone fireplace at one end of the cabin. Behind it, was a chimney that was built out of square, coal-oil cans. Above it, stretched a steel rod from which a kettle could be hung.[276]

Across the end of the cabin was a lean-to shed, which was built out of poles and split Cedar.[277]

Hope Bay in 1946 - Pender Islands Museum

Hope Bay was named after this brother, who was famous for his home-baked bread, which he would set out in the sun to rise.[278]

Hope Bay as it appears today

Hope Bay is located on the east side of North Pender. The rocky beach at Hope Bay is accessible by way of Port Washington Road. (#36 on the map) If you launch a boat from the government wharf, you can travel north to Bricky Bay. However, keep in mind that tides run up to 3 knots.

Alternatively, you can travel across Navy Channel to Mayne Island and then on to Saturna Island, through a fascinating maze of islands and waterways.

HyaShi Cove

In the late 1920's, a retired Japanese-Canadian sea Captain started a herring saltery and fish processing plant in a cove.[279]

Over time, the sea Captain brought other Japanese families to the cove and became the boss of a Japanese camp that was established there.[280]

The saltery operated a fleet of seiners that fished in the Channel. At night, the fishing fleet displayed a spectacle of lights, while it traveled through the water.[281]

The saltery employed a large number of men, of various nationalities, who had a reputation for singing while they worked.[282] As they sang, they packed the fish in cases, salting the fish heavily to escape paying a salt tax. Then, they sold them to countries in the Orient.[283]

At the onset of World War II, when the Japanese-Canadian residents were taken from their homes on the Penders, the saltery was taken over by The London Packers. The plant burned down in the 1950's.[284]

PeNder IsLaNds

Otter Bay in 1946 – Pender Islands Museum

Hyashi Cove was named after the Japanese-Canadian sea Captain who established the saltery.[285] Some remains of its concrete foundation can still be seen there.

The cove sits within a larger body of water, called *Otter Bay*, which is located on the northwest side of North Pender. It provides for the finest sandy beach on the Penders, which is accessible by way

of steep steps off Niagara Road. The steps provide for a seasonal waterfall. (#9 on the map)

The *Otter Bay Marina* at the cove provides for temporary boat anchorage. If you launch a boat from the marina, you can travel south along a fascinating shoreline to Mouat Point. From there, you can continue all the way to Wallace Point. However, there are few places to pull out around Oaks Bluff.

Irene Bay

Irene Bay, on the west side of North Pender, provides for a sandy beach that is accessible from Irene Bay Road. (#10 on the map)

James Point

During World War I, a sea Captain purchased a property, called *Waterlea*, and then gave it to his daughter.[286]

His daughter's husband was the first real estate agent to reside on the Penders. He would provide free room and board in their home, to prospective clients who came to the Island to view properties.[287]

Soon, his daughter became accustomed to providing for her husband's clients. So she converted their home into a resort, taking in guests in the summer.[288]

The resort had several rowboats, a tennis court and a pavilion that extended out over the water. Whenever the couple's children wanted to prevent the guests from using these facilities, they would wait until low tide, and then suggest to the guests that they have a picnic on nearby Betty Island. As a result, the guests would become stranded when the tide came back in.[289]

During the 1930's, the Canadian Pacific Railway steamers would pass by the resort. Sometimes, one of them would stop so guests could disembark. The guests would crowd onto one side of the ship and a rope ladder would be let down.[290]

The family lived at Waterlea until the 1940's.[291] The home can still be seen sitting on a point today.

James Point is located on the west side of North Pender. It has an ecologically sensitive sandy beach that is accessible by way of steps off the end of MacKinnon Road. (#8 on the map)

LittLe Bay

In the late 1880's, the first permanent Penderite was married on a Saturna Island ranch. His bride, who would later become the Postmistress for South Pender, wore a white satin dress that was custom-made in London.[292]

> **Treasure Hunt**
> There is a cairn commemorating a pilot who crashed his plane during World War II. Can you find it on a trail?

After the wedding, the couple began their honeymoon by sailing home, to South Pender, in a war canoe. The father of the bride had hired two Indians to paddle it.[293] Upon landing in a bay, they made their way through the woods to their new home.[294]

Little Bay, on the northeast side of South Pender, provides for views of Mount Warburton Pike on Saturna Island. The rocky beach is accessible by way of two flights of steep steps off Ancia Road. (#25 on the map)

PeNder ISLaNdS

Magic Lake

Much of the population of the Penders is concentrated around its most popular swimming hole. Originally named *Dead Cow Slough*, it is officially named *Pender Lake*, but is known locally as *Magic Lake*.[295]

Magic Lake is located on the southwest side of North Pender, in Magic Lake Estates. It is accessible by way of Pirates Road. (#31 on the map) You can launch a boat in the lake and there are facilities for picnics along the shore if you want to stay awhile.

Medicine Beach

Medicine Beach, at the north end of Bedwell Harbour contains low shell midden from the site of an ancient Coast Salish Indian settlement. The Pender Island Conservancy Association recently purchased the land at Medicine Beach as a wildlife sanctuary.

Two rare species of plants grow in this ecological reserve, which is now protected as one of the few remaining wetlands in the southern Gulf Islands. Great Blue Herons and Kingfishers are plentiful there and there is also the occasional Osprey sighting.

There are three accesses to Medicine Beach; one is off Schooner Way and two are off Wallace Road. (#19 on the map) However, the beach is closed to the harvesting of scallops, mussels, oysters and clams.

PeNder IslaNds

MortiMer Spit

In the 1880's, there was a quarry at the harbour on North Pender. It produced stone that was used to build the tower of Holy Trinity Cathedral on the mainland.[296] When the canal was dredged between North and South Pender at the turn of the century, the dredging started at the site of the abandoned quarry.[297]

Mortimer Spit was named after the company who owned the quarry. It is a sandbar on the most westerly tip of South Pender, which provides for one of the best swimming and clam digging beaches on the Penders. The spit is accessible by way of Canal Road. (#33 on the map)

PaNda Bay

Panda Bay is located on the west side of North Pender, in Magic Lake Estates. A trail off Harpoon Road leads to steps down to a sandy beach. (#13 on the map)

Roe Lake

In the 1890's, a family immigrated to Canada from Scotland.[298] There, they purchased the first Port Washington Community Hall building, as well as the outbuilding that had originally been used as the school. Then, they moved the two buildings together to make themselves a home.[299]

Roe Lake, on the west side of North Pender, was named after this family, who went on to develop the Roesland Resort at the turn of the century. The lake is one of the only natural, freshwater lakes in the Gulf Islands and provides for secluded swimming.

> **Treasure Hunt**
> *There is a rock that bears the date the HMS Egeria landed on South Pender. Can you find it on a beach?*

The easy 2 km trail to Roe Lake wanders through second-growth forest. It is accessible by way of Shingle Bay Road. (#11 on the map)

Walking south along the trail will lead to the trail junction. At the junction, the trail to the left encircles the lake in a clockwise direction.

SHINGLe Bay

At the turn of the century, two brothers purchased a portable sawmill and began to cut boards and shingles[300] out of a fine stand of Western Red Cedar that grew behind a bay.[301] Then, they built a scow and established the first mill ever to exist on the Pender Islands.[302]

The brothers used a steam launch, called *Pearl*, to transport the lumber from the bay. It was the first powerboat ever used on the Penders.[303]

Shingle Bay is located in Shingle Bay Park, on the west side of North Pender. It can be accessed either from Galleon Way or by way of trails on Masthead Crescent and Yardarm Road. (#12 on the map)

SuSaN PoiNt

Susan Point, on the northern tip of North Pender, provides for a short trail that is accessible from Walden Road. (#1 on the map) The trail heads toward steps, which lead down to a pebbled beach.

Teece Point

In the 1930's, The Ranch on South Pender was sold to a married couple who turned it into a thriving poultry business. Later, they sold the business to their son-in-law, but continued to live there as managers, running a herd of fine beef cattle.[304]

Teece Point was named after this couple. Originally named Blunden Point,[305] it is the most easterly tip of South Pender.

A short trail near the end of Boundary Pass Drive leads to steps that descend to the beach. (#26 on the map) At low tide, you can walk to a small, rocky islet off the point.

Thieves Bay

Around the turn of the century, the provincial police learned that two sheep rustlers were killing and salting down sheep at a bay. So the police rounded up a posse of settlers, gave them guns and ammunition, and swore them in as special constables. Then, they all rowed to the bay to arrest the sheep rustlers.[306]

When the posse arrived at the bay, they apprehended the two criminals and handcuffed them. After the settlers went home, the policeman removed the handcuffs from the prisoners and made them do the rowing to the *gaol* (jail) on Mayne Island.[307]

Unfortunately, when they arrived on Mayne, the policeman made the mistake of getting out of the boat first and his prisoners seized the opportunity to push the boat away from the shore. Then, they quickly paddled into the Pass and were never seen again.[308]

Thieves Bay is located in Thieves Bay Park, on the west side of North Pender. It provides for a sandy beach and marina. The beach is accessible by way of two trails off Anchor Way. (#14 on the map)

WaLLace PoiNt

During Prohibition, a point on North Pender became a favorite rendezvous site for liquor runners. They would take shelter on the point whenever they transferred their illegal cargo to boats traveling across the U.S. border.[309]

Wallace Point is the southernmost tip of North Pender. There are three sandy beaches at the end of this very lovely point. (#18 on the map)

The beaches are accessible by way of Trincoma Place, Bedwell Drive and Plumper Way.

WeLcoMe Bay

Welcome Bay is located on the northeast side of North Pender. It provides for views of tiny Fane Island. A trail off Clam Bay Road leads to steps down to a pebbled beach on the bay. (#4 on the map)

WiLdLiFe to ObSerVe

The wildlife found in the southern Gulf Islands is very diverse. The Islands are a great place to watch wildlife and are most spectacular in the spring. Although, many species are commonly seen throughout the year, some are more elusive and it requires a bit of luck to spot them.

Some plant and animal specifies found in the Gulf Islands cannot be found anywhere else in Canada. There are some interesting species of wildlife that are rare and endangered. The rarely seen Sharp-Tailed Snake is known to exist only in the Gulf Islands and on the southeastern portion of Vancouver Island. However, only the most commonly seen species have been listed in this book.

MarINe MaMMaLS

Marine mammals have adapted characteristics to survive and prosper in environments that are hostile to most land mammals. Some migrate from the southern Gulf Islands to tropical habitats that are suitable for birthing. Northern migrations begin early in the spring and southern migrations begin in the fall.

The Orca Pass initiative is a citizen-led project whereby both Canada and the United States have agreed to cooperate on the preservation and protection of the Orca Pass International Stewardship Area. This area is a delicate marine mammal and sea-life environment around the southern Gulf Islands.

Many marine mammals can frequently be seen swimming through Active Pass, the waterway that lies between Galiano and Mayne Islands. It is traveled by ferries on route to Vancouver Island from the mainland.

Harbour Porpoises, or Common Porpoises, are small whales that only grow to 1.8 m in length. They are brown to black in color, with a white underside. They can frequently be seen swimming through Active Pass.

Harbour Seals, also known as Common Seals or Leopard Seals, can grow to 1.8 m in length. They are gray with a unique pattern of fine, dark spots. They have a whiskery nose and bulging eyes. Their hind flippers extend backwards.

There was a Canadian bounty on Harbour Seals for several decades after the turn of the century. However, today, they can be found in quiet, rocky places where they can land during low tide. They are the marine mammals you are most likely to see around the southern Gulf Islands, but they will dive into the water if they are approached too closely. You can often see seals swimming at Hope Bay.

Orcas, also known as Killer Whales, Black Fish or Grampus, are actually dolphins. They are black with a white chest and sides. They sport a white patch above and behind the eye. They can grow to 9.5 m in length and weigh as much as 10,000 kilograms.

The coast of British Columbia is well known as the place on *Elehe* (Earth) to watch migrating and resident orcas feeding and breaching. Resident orcas are almost exclusively fish eaters.

However, transient orcas eat seals, sea lion pups, birds, and even porpoises and dolphins if they can catch them.

At the time of this writing, there were 81 resident orcas in the southern Gulf Islands, as well as the San Juan Islands and Washington State. They are usually seen in pods of 5-25 animals.

Pacific White-Sided Dolphin are greenish-black with a white belly and grey stripes along their sides. They can grow to a length of 2.5 m. Large groups of dolphin readily approach boats in Active Pass in the spring and fall. Fishermen often refer to them as 'lags'.

Sea Lions can grow to 3 m in length and weigh up to 1,000 kg. They are brown to black in color. Some species were put on the U.S. endangered species list and have since been the object of intense study. Some species are intelligent and adaptable, and are often trained as entertainers at ocean parks and zoos.

PeNder ISLaNdS

Around the southern Gulf Islands, sea lions delight in throwing kelp around and body surfing the waves.

Otters are reddish-brown to black in color. They are intelligent and very playful, frequently floating and swimming on their backs.

Otters became extinct in British Columbia in the 1920's. In the 1960's, 89 otters were reintroduced from Alaska and have begun to spread again, along the west coast of Vancouver Island.

Sea LiFe

The ocean environment around the southern Gulf Islands supports a delicate, yet complex web of life. When the tide recedes, the depressions that retain water between the rocks are called *tidal pools*, which are natural aquariums for an abundance of vertebrates and invertebrates. *Siwash loggers* (beachcombers) can see this life when the tide goes out.

For those who want to gather filter-feeding shellfish from around the southern Gulf Islands, a permit is required to dig and quantities are limited.

Clams, or Macoma, can live for 20 years or more. Although the Smooth Washington Clam is the mainstay of the clam business, there are several varieties around the southern Gulf Islands, most of which are white in color.

If you find a clam shell on the beach surface, the clam is no longer living in it. However, finding live *luk'-ut-chee* (clams) is not difficult if you look in mixed mud, rock and sand. The smallest clams, called *Little-Necks*, can be found just beneath the surface. The larger *Butter Clams*, which can live for 20 years, can be found about 20 cm from the surface. The largest and longest-living clams, called *Horse Clams*, can be found about 30 cm from the surface.

Clams feed, breathe and expel waste through tubes that extend up to the surface of the beach. You can tell if there are clams embedded in a beach if you see water squirting out of the sand. A small shovel or hand rake works well to uncover them.

Crabs are reddish-brown to purple in color. Some species of crab can grow to a width of 23 cm and can live for 6 years.

You need a trap to actually land crabs that are large enough to eat and catching crabs is a secret kept by *island crabbers* (Gulf Islanders who catch crab). However, because they prefer a sand or mud ocean bottom, you can see small specimens in shallow waters. In fact, most of the movement you see in tidal pools are crabs scurrying about.

Cockles look somewhat like clams. They are cream-colored with a grey or brown mottled pattern. They have deeply set ridges, which make them easy to identify.

Cockles can often be found on or near the surface of muddy or sandy beaches. Some species can live for up to 16 years.

Jellyfish are not actually fish. They are a member of the invertebrate family. They feed on small fish and zooplankton that become caught in their tentacles where their stinging cells latch onto them. They are usually found floating near the surface of the water or stranded on the beach.

Limpets have an elliptical shell that rises to a peak. Unlike mussels, clams and oysters, limpets have only one shell half, which is usually greenish brown with cream lines radiating down from the peak. The underside has a brown spot in the center.

Limpets can be found attached to the sides of the rocks along the shoreline on the beach.

Mussels found on the southern Gulf Islands are generally dark blue with hints of brown. They can grow to 20 cm in length. They attach themselves to rocks and to wood, especially to pilings.

To gather *to'-luks* (mussels), just locate a colony and pry them loose. As you gather them, make sure the shells are closed tightly or that they snap shut when you grab them.

Oysters are greyish-white in color. Their shells are wavy and mold to the object they attach themselves to. They can grow to 30 cm in length. The Japanese introduced some of the oysters to the southern Gulf Islands, in the 1920's.

The *klógh-klogh* (oyster) can be found attached to rocks on the beach surface. To gather them, you must pry them loose with a sharp tool. If you harvest a supply of oysters, consider leaving the shells on the beach for new generations of oysters.

Sea Stars, or Starfish, around the southern Gulf Islands are usually purple in color, but can also be a bright coral color. They can grow to over 36 cm in diameter.

Sea Stars are carnivores that feed on mussels and barnacles. They flip their

stomach out through their mouth and digest their prey from the inside out.

It is not uncommon to see a Sea Star with a partially regenerated limb. If they lose a limb, they can regenerate it.[310]

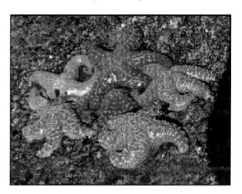

Snails have long, cylindrical-shaped shells that are gray to brown in color. The shell often has a stripe winding around it. They only grow to 3 cm, but they can live for 10 years. You can find them in shallow water. The Japanese accidentally introduced some species of snails to the Gulf Islands, in the 1920's.

LaNd MaMMaLS

Hunting is no longer permitted in the Gulf Islands, except by bow and arrow. Because of that, the land mammals that live there are relatively tame.

Columbia Blacktail Deer, or Mowich, are a small sub-species of mule deer. They are the largest land mammals you are likely to see on the southern Gulf Islands.

A major difference between the Columbian Blacktail and other deer is in the way they can leap, and then land with all four legs hitting the ground at the same time. This enables them to change direction in one bound.

You can identify the seasons by the development of a buck's antlers. In the spring, the buds appear on his head. In summer, he grows lush velvet, which coats the antlers. In the fall, the velvet falls off, hardening the antler bone underneath. In winter, the antlers are cast off.

Unfortunately, as cute as they are, deer eliminate the forest understory in their search for food and are widespread enough to support the outer Gulf Islands' fence builders. You can find them just about everywhere.

Douglas Squirrels, or Chickaree, are brown rodents with a bushy tail and a distinctive call. They make their home in tree cavities or in nests constructed of twigs, needles and bark. You can see them leaping from branch to branch in the dense forests around the Penders.

Raccoons have soft, dense, grey fur and a black mask across their face. They have long tails that are characterized by a pattern of rings. You can see raccoons along some of the beaches around the southern Gulf Islands. Their presence is revealed by human-like handprints, which can be seen in the mud.

Townsend's Chipmunks are brown rodents with black stripes. They hibernate during the winter months.

However, in the summer, because they seldom climb trees, they can be seen scurrying along the ground in the dense forests around the Penders.

BirdS

The southern Gulf Islands are well known for their bird watching opportunities. The rocky shores are stopover sites for migratory birds and nesting sites for many sea birds.

Over 130 species of marine birds from 22 countries breed, migrate and/or spend the winter in the Strait. Because the climate invites them to reside or visit, the southern Gulf Islands become a *kalakala* (bird) watchers' paradise in the winter.

Bald Eagles have a white head and tail, and a contrasting brown body. They can grow to 90 cm tall with a wingspan of 2 m. Although they are indigenous to North America, they were on the brink of extinction late in the 20th century. Fortunately, they have largely recovered and, today, 25 percent of the world's

eagle nesting population is found in British Columbia.

Eagles are birds of prey. Their main food supply is the Glaucous-Winged Gull. In the summer, they search for surface-feeding fish, snatching food with aerial acrobatics. They are also good at forcing other birds to drop their prey and will often steal prey from an Osprey.

'Baldies' are commonly seen around the southern Gulf Islands, especially in the spring when they are rearing their young. Those that are old enough to nest often return to the area in which they were raised. Their nests, which are protected by law, can span 3 m across and weigh 900 kg. They eventually collapse under their own weight.

Because they prefer nest sites with a view, you can see them in Lilias Spalding Heritage Park and at Hope Bay.

Belted Kingfishers have deep blue or bluish-gray plumage with white markings. The blue feathers on their heads make their heads appear larger than they are. They have a broad, white collar around their neck and a blue band around their chest. The female has an orange band, as well. As loners, they only tolerate one another at mating time.

The Belted Kingfisher is the only species of kingfisher found in the Pacific Northwest. Whenever there is good fishing around the southern Gulf Islands, you can expect to find them perched on trees or posts, close to the water on Medicine Beach. They are a noisy bird with a loud, rattling call. On a calm winter day, the kingfisher's call can often be heard across Hope Bay.

Brown Creepers have a mottled brown coloration and long, stiff tail-feathers. Their cheerful song has been described as 'trees, trees, trees, see the trees'.

Brown Creepers are common, year-round residents of the forests on the Islands. A creeper will typically forage upwards on tree bark. As it nears the treetop, it drops to the base of a nearby tree to begin its ascent all over again. If it is frightened, it will flatten itself against the tree trunk, becoming almost impossible to see.

Canada Geese have a black head and neck. They have a broad, white chin strap with a contrasting brown body. In flight, they slice through the skies in 'V-formations' or in long lines.

Canada Geese mate for life and are faithful to their breeding grounds, returning to their birth sites each spring. They are abundant waterfowl that can be found year-round.

Cormorants are dark, long-necked, diving birds with long bills. They often stand upright and hold their wings out to dry. They can be seen flying in single file, floating low in the water, or hanging out on rocks or pilings at Hope Bay.

Great Blue Herons, also known as a Shagpoke or Shikspoke, are long-legged, greyish-blue, wading birds. They can grow to 1.2 m tall with a 2 m wingspan. They have a plume of black feathers behind their eye.

Great Blue Herons can be seen standing like sentinels, gazing into the water at low tide, in search of food. They feed in shallow water and spear fish or frogs with their long, sharp bills. They will also raid goldfish ponds in Islanders' backyards. You can hear them croak as they fly laboriously to their enormous nests of sticks.

The herons found on the southern Gulf Islands are a distinctive subspecies. They are year-round residents. You can find them on Medicine Beach and at Hope Bay.

Grouse generally have a brown camouflage pattern. Some species are

so well camouflaged that they allow humans, and even predators, to approach very closely. Grouse are year-round, ground-dwelling residents of the Islands' forests. First Nations used to hunt grouse so they could boil them in a soup.

Gulls are graceful in flight, voracious when feeding and capable of many sounds. One small, delicate species is most often seen around the southern Gulf Islands in winter. However, other species can be found, year-round, particularly at Hope Bay.

Ospreys are mostly white underneath, with contrasting dark coloration above. They display a dark line through their eye. Most Ospreys depart the southern Gulf Islands in the fall and return in the spring. You can find them along the shoreline on Medicine Beach and at Hope Bay.

Ospreys are aggressors and birds of prey. An Osprey will attack an eagle if it comes too close to its nest.

When an Osprey sees a fish in the water, it will suddenly tuck in its wings and plummet down, throwing its feet forward at the last minute. It will then grasp the fish with its talons and carry it with its head forward, to cut down on wind resistance. For this reason, some people refer to them as 'fish hawks'.

Pacific Loons are dark brown with a white belly. In winter, they display a border between the front and the back of their neck. This changes in the summer when they display a velvety grey head, a dark throat and a checkered back.

Pacific Loons are dark brown with a white belly. They are diving birds, preferring areas of *skookumchuck* (strong currents), where they dive for fish. Sometimes, in the spring, hundreds of them can be seen diving in Active Pass. In summer, they display a velvety grey head, a dark throat and a checkered back.

In winter, Pacific Loons display a border between the front and the back of their neck. Some of North America's largest wintering population exists on the southern Gulf Islands. They arrive in the fall from their northern breeding grounds.

Red-Breasted Nuthatches are small, short-tailed birds with sharp beaks. They have a black cap with a white eye-stripe and a bit of rusty coloring on their chest. When they are building a nest, their hammering can sound like that of a woodpecker.

Unlike the Brown Creeper, nuthatches spiral down tree trunks, headfirst, pulling insects out of the bark. They will stay close to home year-round if there is enough food or a bird feeder in the area. They can be found in the mature, cone-bearing forests around the southern Gulf Islands, where their call is a familiar sound.

Red-Tailed Hawks have broad wings and a broad, rust-colored tail. They are designed for soaring on thermals of warm, rising air. They are birds of prey and will eat almost any small animal. The blood-curdling scream of a Red-Tailed Hawk is what is often heard in the movies. They can be found virtually everywhere on the southern Gulf Islands, year-round.

Rufous Hummingbirds can fly left, right, up, down, backwards and even upside down. When hovering, they hold their bodies upright and flap their wings horizontally in a 'figure eight'. Most 'hummers' flap their wings 12,000 times per minute, which is why they are seen as a blur.

Rufous Hummingbirds must eat half their weight in sugar each day. In early spring, they leave their wintering grounds in Mexico and make their way north, flower-by-flower, sucking the nectar from the bloom of the Red-Flowering Currant and Salmonberry shrubs. A long, stiletto bill assists them in this lifestyle. They can be found in the Islands' forests and gardens.

Steller's Jays are the avian emblem of British Columbia. They are deep bluish-black in color and are frequently mistaken for the eastern Blue Jay. They have a dark crest that raises and lowers to indicate their state of agitation.

Announcing their arrival with a raucous call, Steller's Jays will descend upon a bird feeder, scattering smaller birds from it. As year-round residents that live on the Islands' forest slopes, they also like to grab acorns from trees, such as Garry Oak.

Swallows winter in South America and are seen on the southern Gulf Islands in the summer. Several varieties exist, ranging in color from blue to green to brown to purple.

In the last half of the 20th century, the population of Western Purple Martins, the largest species in the swallow family, has declined drastically. Since the 1980's, the Georgia Basin Ecological Assessment and Restoration Society has helped the population recover by installing more than 1,100 nest boxes throughout the Strait. Young Purple Martins see the nest boxes and return to them each spring.[311]

Turkey Vultures have two-toned wings and a naked, red head. They are birds of prey that are usually seen in flight with wings in a 'V-formation'. Their tilting flight is an energy-saving strategy. Without turning it's head, a Turkey Vulture can see views of the land below. It will spiral upwards within a thermal of warm, rising air, then descend in a long glide to catch the next thermal.

In the fall, Turkey Vultures use the southern Gulf Islands as stepping stones as they head south to California and Mexico. One of the best places to find them is perched in the trees in Lilias Spalding Heritage Park.

PLaceS to FiSH

Gulf Island waters are renowned throughout North America for their salmon, bottom fish and shellfish. Active Pass is a prized salmon-fishing ground, providing the best summer fishing in the Gulf Islands and salmon fishing in the Georgia Strait is a year-round sport, with the best fishing occurring in winter.

Active Pass is famous for some of the greatest Spring and Coho salmon fishing in the world. It is a crossroads for salmon returning to spawn in the Fraser River, which has the world's largest, natural, salmon runs. Keep in mind that the excellent fishing occurs there during months when the ferry traffic is at its highest, and accidents between ferries and sport fishermen have occurred there.

Porlier Pass, off the north side of Galiano, is also known for its salmon fishing. However, tides in Porlier Pass run up to 9 knots and are dangerous to small boats.

Some of the finest salmon fishing in the Gulf Islands is off East Point, on the east side on Saturna Island. It is fished throughout the summer by anglers from both sides of the Strait.

Home to sea-run Cutthroat Trout, Chum and Coho Salmon, Lyall Creek, on Saturna Island, has unusually high numbers of fish for the region and provides for good fishing off the mouth of Lyall Harbour.

You can also fish for salmon off the rocks at Bellhouse Provincial Park, on south Galiano, and between St. John Point and Conconi Reef, on Mayne Island.

If the salmon fishing is slow, you can try fishing for other bottom fish, such as Ling Cod, Red Snapper, Black Bass and Sole.

Razor PoiNt Boat CHarters

Razor Point Boat Charters provides for a charter fishing and sightseeing vessel, with a veteran commercial fisherman as a guide. The boat can accommodate up to four people. The charter company is located on Razor Point Road. Phone: (250) 629-9922

Sporades Tours

Sporades Tours, on Galiano Island, provides for fishing charters in the Gulf Islands. Phone: 1-877-588 3506

Creatures to Cook

In the gold-mining camps of the late 1800's, an expensive egg omelet, called the *Hangtown Fry*, was prepared for hungry gold miners. It contained fried breaded oysters and bacon.[312]

Seafood is incredibly easy to prepare. With a little basic knowledge, you can become an expert in no time at all. The most important thing to remember when cooking seafood is not to overcook it. It is also very important to pay strict attention to the health advisories, as paralytic shellfish poisoning is potentially deadly.

FiSH

The freshness and flavor of a fish, such as salmon, cod and sole, can be preserved all day by killing it immediately and keeping it cool. To clean the fish, simply slice it lengthwise and remove the gills, as well as the contents of the carcass. Then, wash the fish before wrapping it in paper.

After the fish has been cleaned, cut through the backbone so you can *butterfly it* (spread the two sides down) on a grill or frying pan. Simmer the fish over low heat until the bones can be pulled away from the meat.

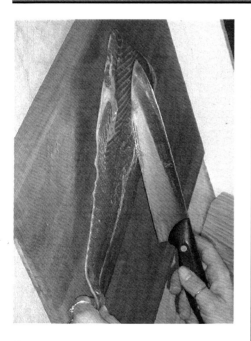

Crab

A crab should be kept alive until it is time to cook it. Before you cook a crab, first remove its shell. To remove the shell, point the crab away from your body, and grasp its legs and pinchers with your hands facing up. Hit it against a hard surface so the top of its shell lifts off. Then, simply break the crab in half and discard the contents of the carcass. To cook the carcass, just boil it and serve it with melted butter for dipping.

CLaMS aNd MuSSeLS

To cook clams or mussels, just drop them into a pot of boiling water and leave them until their shells open.

Discard the green substance from the shells of the clams. Once they have been removed from their shells, you can fry them in butter, or cook them in a pot with bacon, potatoes and milk.

OySters

It is best to *shuck* (open) oysters right on the beach and leave the shells there for new generations of oysters. Shucked oysters can then be fried with Worcestershire sauce or added to a chowder. They can even be eaten raw.

If you prefer to cook your oysters, just throw them on hot coals with the cupped half of the shell up and leave them until their shells open.

FLora to Appreciate

The unique environment in the southern Gulf Islands is host to a wide diversity of plant life. The flora is probably the most varied in all of British Columbia.

The islands sit in one of the smallest climate zones in the west, where the rain shadow holds rainfall to less than 75 cm annually. This climate zone is noted for its beautiful, spring, wild *kloshe tupso* (flowers), over 250 of which grow and flourish on the southern

Gulf Islands - too many to list in this little book.

Trees

The southern Gulf Islands are part of the coastal, Douglas-Fir, plant community, which is marked by the predominance of Douglas-Fir, Arbutus and Garry Oak. This community has a very limited range, which includes only the southern Gulf Islands, Washington State and part of Vancouver Island.

Amabilis means *lovely*. The Amabilis Fir, or Silver Fir, is a tall, straight tree that can grow to 55 m in height. It has flat needles that are dark and shiny, with white lines underneath.

Arbutus, or Madrona, are Canada's only native, broad-leaved evergreen and exist on only a very small portion of the extreme West Coast. They are indigenous to the southern Gulf Islands.

The unusual Arbutus tree produces bright red berries. It sheds its thin, smooth, cinnamon-colored bark. Although they are deciduous, Arbutus do not drop their leaves in the winter.

First Nations believe that the survivors of the *Great Flood* used the Arbutus tree to anchor their canoe to the top of Mount Newton on Vancouver Island.

Bitter Cherry is a small tree that produces pinkish flowers. The flowers develop into bright red, bitter cherries. First Nations peeled off the stringy bark of the Bitter Cherry for wrapping harpoon and arrow joints.

Black Cottonwood is a hardy tree with a straight trunk. It can grow to 50 m tall. It has large, sticky, fragrant buds. The

Black Cottonwood is named for the white hairs on its seeds, which float through the air like wisps of cotton.

First Nations made canoes from cottonwood trees. Some tribes produced soap from the inner bark. The Hudson's Bay Company reportedly continued using this method in their own brand of soaps.

Black Hawthorn is a small tree that produces white flowers. The flowers develop into small, edible, blackish-purple fruits that are shaped like apples. The thorns of the Black Hawthorn were used by First Nations as game pieces when playing games.

Broadleaf Maple, or Bigleaf Maple, is the largest maple tree in Canada, reaching heights of 36 m. Its leaves measure up to 30 cm across. It is restricted to the southwest corner of British Columbia.

First Nations called the Broadleaf Maple the *Paddle Tree* because they made paddles out of the wood.

Cascara is a small tree that produces small, greenish-yellow flowers that develop into bluish-black berries. First Nations boiled the bark of the cascara into a tea that was drank as a strong laxative.

Douglas-Fir, also known as the Oregon Pine or Nootka Pine, is the dominant species of tree on the southern Gulf Islands. It can be found just about everywhere. It can grow to 85 m high and 2 m wide. Its bark is very thick and deeply grooved.

First Nations had many uses for Douglas-Fir. They used it to make fish hooks and handles. They used the wood and boughs as fuel for cooking. Its boughs were frequently used for covering the floors of lodges.

The Grand Fir is also found on the southern Gulf Islands. It is easily distinguished from other fir trees by its flat needle sprays that grow in two rows.

Garry Oaks, or Oregon White Oaks, are picturesque, gnarled, hardwood trees. They can grow to 20 m in height and can live for up to 500 years. Oaks have thick, grooved, greyish-black bark. They produce small acorns with a scaly cup on one end.

In Canada, Garry Oak are found almost exclusively on southeastern portion of Vancouver Island, and on the southern Gulf Islands. Unfortunately, their numbers are in decline throughout the range.

Typically, the Garry Oak forms open parkland and meadows. However, from the time the southern Gulf Islands were first settled until the 1950's, much of the land that contained the oak was either logged or converted to farms.

Cone-bearing trees grow faster than Garry Oak. This creates shade where the oak cannot regenerate. Although you can find small examples of Garry Oak on the southern Gulf Islands, less than five percent of the original Garry Oak habitat remains. One of the best places in the outer Gulf Islands to see Garry Oak is at Beaumont Provincial Marine Park.

Lodgepole Pine trees are commonly cut down for Christmas trees. They can grow to 40 m in height. Their cones often remain closed for years and open from the heat of a fire. This allows them to develop rapidly after a forest fire.

The Western White Pine is also found on the southern Gulf Islands. It is a symmetrical tree that can grow to 40 m in height, or taller. It is a five-needle pine. First Nations called it the *Dancing Tree*. They boiled its bark into a tea, which they drank to treat tuberculosis and rheumatism.

In the early 1900's, a shipment of Eastern White Pine was imported to the mainland from France. It carried a fungus called White Pine Blister Rust, which kills young Western White Pine trees. The fungus spread to the southern Gulf Islands so quickly that, by the 1920's, it was established throughout most of the tree range.[313]

Pacific Crabapple trees produce pinkish, fragrant, apple blossoms. The blossoms develop into small, reddish apples that are somewhat tart. During preservation, the apples become sweeter.

Pacific Dogwood is an irregular tree that produces white flowers with purple tips. The flowers develop into clusters of bright red berries. The blossom of the dogwood is the floral emblem of British Columbia.

Pacific Dogwood is one of the few plants protected by law in British Columbia. However, in spite of its protection, it has often been illegally cut down.

Pacific Willow are tall, slender trees with pale yellow leaves associated with a flower. Although they only grow to 12 m tall, they are one of the largest native willows on the West Coast.

Red Alder is an aggressive, fast-growing hardwood tree that does not live much past 50 years. The wood of the alder provides one of the best fuels for smoking fish.

Sitka Spruce, or Airplane Spruce, are large trees that commonly grow to 70 m tall and 2 m across. First Nations fashioned watertight hats and baskets from the roots, which also provided materials for ropes and fishing line.

Western Hemlock is a large tree that can grow to 50 m tall. It has sweeping branches and feathery foliage. Unfortunately, its shallow rooting system makes it susceptible to being blown over by wind. Because its wood is very easy to work with, some First Nations carved it into dishes.

Mountain Hemlock also grows on the southern Gulf Islands. It has drooping branches that have an upward sweep at the tip. In dense forests, its needles form flat sprays.

Western Red Cedar, or Canoe Cedar, is British Columbia's official tree. It is very aromatic and has graceful, swooping branches. The cedar can grow to 60 m tall and its trunk spreads widely at its base.

The cedar was considered the *Tree Of Life* by the First Nations who used its wood for dugout canoes, boxes, tools and paddles. From the inner bark, they made rope, clothing, and baskets. Most of their dwellings were constructed of large boards split from cedar logs.

Western Red Cedars live a long life, sometimes to over 1,000 years. As a result, they can be found just about everywhere on the southern Gulf Islands. The Yellow-Cedar is also found on the southern Gulf Islands. It is the oldest tree in the area. Some are 1,500 years old. However, unlike the Western Red Cedar, the crushed leaves of the Yellow-Cedar smell like mildew.

Western Yew, or Pacific Yew, is a small evergreen tree that has reddish, papery bark. Its trunk is often twisted and fluted. Although the yew is a cone-bearing tree, it produces a single seed. A bright red, fleshy cup, which looks like a large berry, surrounds the seed. Beware of the seed, as it is poisonous.

The tough wood of the Western Yew was highly prized by First Nations. Because it displays a polished surface, it was used for carving.

SHrubS aNd FerNS

A characteristic feature of the shrubs on the southern Gulf Islands is the variety and abundance that exist in the Heather family. These shrubs dominate the understory of the Islands' mature forests, as well as in non-forested habitats. Many of the shrubs give way to edible *olali* (berries). First Nations ate these berries raw or boiled into cakes.

Black Raspberry, or Blackcap, is an erect shrub that has stems with curved prickles. It produces pinkish flowers that develop into hairy, purplish-black berries that are very tasty.

Black Twinberry, or Bearberry Honeysuckle, is an erect to straggly shrub. It produces yellow, tubular flowers, which develop into pairs of shiny, black, inedible berries.

Bog Cranberry is a dwarf shrub that only grows to 40 cm tall. It produces deep pink flowers that have petals that bend backwards. Its berries are pale pink to dark red in color.

Bracken Fern has a stout stem with a feathery frond. Its fronds were used by First Nations as a protective layer in food storage containers, on berry-drying racks and in pit ovens.

Copperbush is a leafy shrub with loose, shredding, copper-colored bark. Its flowers are also copper-colored. Its fruit develop as round capsules. It is one of only a few of the plants in its classification found exclusively in Western North America.

Devil's Club is an erect to sprawling shrub. It has thick, crooked stems that are often entangled and armed with numerous, large, yellowish spines. The wood of the shrub has a sweet smell. Its leaves are shaped like that of a maple leaf and it produces white flowers.

Related to the Ginseng plant, Devil's Club is one of the most important of all medicinal plants. Sticks made from Devil's Club were used by First Nations as protective charms. When burned, the charcoal from this shrub was used to make face paint for dancers and for tattoo ink.

Dull Oregon Grape is a common, low-growing evergreen shrub with leaves that resemble that of holly. Bright yellow flowers appear in the spring, followed by dark purple, edible berries in the summer. The berries make great jelly. Tall Oregon Grape is another shrub that can be found on the southern Gulf Islands, but in drier areas.

Evergreen Huckleberry has branches that bear leathery leaves lined with sharp teeth. Its clusters of pink flowers produce black berries with a flavor similar to that of a blueberry. Black Mountain Huckleberry is also found on the southern Gulf Islands. It thrives in old burned sites that have only sparse tree regeneration. You can find huckleberry on Campbell Point.

False Azalea, or False Huckleberry, is an erect to straggly, spreading shrub, which resembles both the Azalea plant, as well as huckleberry plants. It produces pink to yellow flowers, which develop into inedible fruit. The leaves turn a bright crimson color in the fall.

False Box is a low, dense, evergreen shrub that resembles the Kinnikinnick plant. It produces tiny, maroon colored flowers that have a pleasant fragrance. It has reddish-brown branches that are often used in floral arrangements.

Goats' Beard, or Spaghetti Flower, is a robust rose bush. It produces white flower clusters that resemble goats' beards. First Nations used the roots for medicinal purposes.

Gummy Gooseberry is an erect to spreading shrub with sticky leaves. It produces reddish colored flowers in drooping clusters. Its flowers, which produce nectar that is eaten by hummingbirds, develop into dark purple, hairy berries. The Wild Gooseberry, which produces green or purple flowers, can also be found on the southern Gulf Islands.

Gorse is a non-native shrub with vicious spines that can form impenetrable thickets. Unlike most plants that grow poorly in soils low in nitrogen, it can remove nitrogen from the air. This enables it to thrive in soils that are low in nitrogen. Gorse is a fire hazard.

Hairy Manzanita is an erect or spreading evergreen with very hairy leaves. Its branches have reddish-brown bark that peels. It produces pinkish flowers in hairy clusters. Manzanita means *little apples*, which describes its edible, coffee colored berries.

Hardhack, or Steeplebush, is an erect, leggy shrub with many woolly branches. It produces rose colored flowers in a long, narrow cluster. Its fruit develop as clusters of numerous, small, pod-like follicles.

Himalayan Blackberry is an immigrant species from India, which was brought to North America in the 1880's. It has sharp, curved spines that make this precursor of barbed wire a plant to be treated with respect. Gulf Islanders pull the deadly branches towards them using a straightened coat hanger.

Himalayan Blackberry produces fine white or pink flowers. The fruit, which is a favorite among berry pickers, is easily mistaken for a raspberry. However, unlike the blackberry, the fruit of the raspberry is hollow when picked.

The Himalayan Blackberry grows in abundance on the southern Gulf Islands.

Indian-Plum, or Osoberry, is a tall shrub with purplish-brown bark. It is one of the first plants to flower in the spring, at which time it produces greenish-white flowers in long clusters. Its flowers, which have an unusual scent, are produced before its leaves appear. Its fruit, which is often referred to as *choke-cherries*, resembles small plums.

Kinnikinnick, or Common Bearberry, is a creeping, evergreen, ground cover that forms dense mats. It has small, pinkish flowers. The flowers produce bright red, berries that resemble miniature apples.

Mock Orange is an erect shrub with peeling bark. It produces broad, white, fragrant flowers that develop into oval, woody fruit. First Nations used the wood for making bows and arrows.

Ocean Spray, also called Creambush or Ironwood, is an erect shrub with peeling bark. It produces creamy flowers in dense clusters that resemble lilacs. The flowers remain on the plant over the winter. The strong wood of the shrub was used by First Nations to make knitting needles and other tools.

Orange Honeysuckle, also called Ghost's Swing or Owl's Swing, is a climbing vine that can reach 6 m in height. It produces long, orange, trumpet-shaped flowers with a sweet nectar deep inside. Because they can reach into the flower to suck its nectar, they are a favorite of hummingbirds.

The fruit of the Orange Honeysuckle develop as bunches of translucent, orange berries. Coastal Indian children also liked to suck the nectar from the base of the honeysuckle flower.

Pacific Ninebark is an erect to spreading shrub with what is believed to be nine layers of peeling bark. It produces small, white flowers that develop into reddish bunches of fruit. First Nations made knitting needles from the wood.

Red Flowering Currant is a tall, erect shrub. It produces white to red flowers in drooping clusters that indicate the beginning of spring. The flowers, which attract hummingbirds, develop into bluish-black berries that are edible, but not very tasty.

Red Elderberry, or Red Elder, is a tall shrub that can grow to 6 m. It produces clusters of creamy flowers with a strong, unpleasant odor. The flowers develop into bright red fruit. Blue Elderberry, which produces blue fruit, can also be found on the southern Gulf Islands.

Red-Osier Dogwood is a spreading shrub that can grow to 6 m tall. The branches are often bright red in color. It produces small clusters of greenish flowers, which develop into bluish-white fruit. Although the fruit is very bitter, dogwood is a very important source of food for the deer on the southern Gulf Islands.

Salal means *this plentiful shrub*. This is for good reason, as it is probably the most dominant shrub in the Islands' forests. Salal is an upright or ground crawling plant that can grow sparsely or form a dense barrier that is almost impossible to penetrate. It spreads by suckering layer upon layer.

Salal produces pink flowers that give way to bluish-black berries. The berries, which are juicy, sweet and aromatic, make excellent jams, jellies and wine.

Salmonberry is a branching shrub that often forms dense thickets. It produces pink, red or purple flowers. The flowers develop into mushy, edible, yellow or salmon colored berries. The berries of the Salmonberry are one of the earliest berries to ripen in the spring.

Scotch Broom is a bushy shrub with long, thin stems from which sprout yellow flowers in the spring and pea-shaped pods in the summer.

In the mid-1800's, a European sea captain was immigrating to Vancouver

Island. He brought with him some Scotch Broom seeds that he had picked up from the Hawaiian Islands. Like Gorse, broom can remove the nitrogen it needs from the air, so when the first white settlers began to arrive, it quickly invaded the southern Gulf Islands.[314]

Today, Scotch Broom grows in abundance on the southern Gulf Islands. It produces a toxin that can depress the heart and nervous system. It is also a fire hazard.

Gulf Islanders can often be seen participating in a *Broom Bash* whereby Broom is destroyed in a designated area. The bash is jokingly referred to as an `invasive species removal party`.

Sitka Alder is a tall shrub that can grow to 5 m. It produces a spike-like flower cluster. It also produces clusters of cones from which tiny nuts can be shaken.

Sitka Mountain Ash is an erect shrub that produces small, white clusters of flowers. Its red, berry-like fruits are edible, but very bitter.

Stink Currant is an erect shrub with a skunky smell. It produces greenish clusters of flowers that develop into long clusters of edible, bluish-black berries.

Soopolallie, also called Soapberry or Canadian Buffalo-Berry, is a spreading shrub with branches that are covered with scabs. It produces yellowish-brown flowers. Its bright red berries, which feel soapy to the touch, were used by First Nations to make ice cream.

Sword-Fern, also known as the Pala-Pala plant, is one of the most abundant of the ferns found on the southern Gulf Islands. It is often found growing, along with Western Red Cedar, in damp shady forests. Deer Fern, which resembles the Sword-Fern, also grows on the southern Gulf Islands.

White-Flowered Rhododendron is a slender, erect shrub with peeling bark. It produces clusters of creamy, cup-shaped flowers. Rhododendron is often found along with the False Azalea and Copperbush plants.

Credits

Historical Photos

British Columbia Archives and Records Services

Royal British Columbia Museum

British Columbia Ferry Services Archives

Salt Spring Archives

Galiano Museum & Archives

Pender Islands Museum Society

David Spalding, South Pender Island

Hope Bay Rising Holdings Ltd.

Current Photos

Dreamstime™
Tony Campbell, David Coleman, Galina Barskaya, Paul Wolf, Scott Pehrson, Marilyn Barbone, Steffen Foerster, Steve Degenhardt, Melissa King, Randy McKown, Kutt Niinepuu, Dennis Sabo, Jason Cheever, Ryan Tacay, Costin Cojocaru, Marilyna Barbone, Nick Stubbs

Georgia Strait Alliance
Orca Pass International Stewardship Area

Gulf Islands Water Taxi
Water Taxis

Harbour Air
Beaver Planes

Pender Island Taxi & Tours
Pender Island Taxis

The Pender Islands Artisan Co-Op
Rembrandt's Birthday Art Show, Christmas Craft Fair Exhibit

Stella Roberts
Garden Party

Greg Gerke
Easter Egg Hunt

The Author

Vicky Lindholm moved with her husband to Mayne Island, in December of 2004. Having authored over 30 pieces of computer courseware, she brought with her more than 20 years of writing experience.

Pender Islands: Facts And Folklore is the second book of its kind to be written by this author, who reviewed over 50 existing pieces of literature and explored parks, beaches and wildlife in order to produce this historical view of the Pender Islands. The book is an historical guide to the events, landmarks, parks, beaches, shops, restaurants and wildlife on the Penders. It includes over 200 photos, past to present, most of which the author and her husband photographed themselves.

Vicky currently lives and works on Mayne Island. In addition to making a living as a writer, she manages a small gift ctore, as a home-based business, from her residential property.

Notes

[1] **More Tales from the Outer Gulf Islands:** An Anthology of Memories and Anecdotes – British Columbia Historical Association, pp. 24

[2] **A Gulf Islands Patchwork:** Some Early Events on the Islands of Galiano, Mayne, Saturna, North and South Pender – British Columbia Historical Association, pp. 19 and **More Tales from the Outer Gulf Islands:** An Anthology of Memories and Anecdotes – British Columbia Historical Association, pp. 22, 24 & 26

[3] **Island Heritage Buildings** – Thomas K. Ovanin, Islands Trust, pp. 134

[4] **More Tales from the Outer Gulf Islands:** An Anthology of Memories and Anecdotes – British Columbia Historical Association, pp. 26

[5] **Island Heritage Buildings** – Thomas K. Ovanin, Islands Trust, pp. 134

[6] **More Tales from the Outer Gulf Islands:** An Anthology of Memories and Anecdotes – British Columbia Historical Association, pp. 36

[7] **A Gulf Islands Patchwork:** Some Early Events on the Islands of Galiano, Mayne, Saturna, North and South Pender – British Columbia Historical Association, pp. 21

[8] **More Tales from the Outer Gulf Islands:** An Anthology of Memories and Anecdotes – British Columbia Historical Association, pp. 56

[9] **The Gulf Islanders:** Sound Heritage, Volume V, Number 4, pp. 12

[10] **More Tales from the Outer Gulf Islands:** An Anthology of Memories and Anecdotes – British Columbia Historical Association, pp. 24

[11] **A Gulf Islands Patchwork:** Some Early Events on the Islands of Galiano, Pender, Saturna, North and South Pender – British Columbia Historical Association, pp. 131

[12] **The Pender Post**: Celebrating the activities of the people of Pender Island at the Millennium, The Pender Post Society, pp. 7

[13] **Mayne Island & The Outer Gulf Islands:** A History – Marie Elliott, pp. 79

[14] **A Gulf Islands Patchwork:** Some Early Events on the Islands of Galiano, Pender, Saturna, North and South Pender – British Columbia Historical Association, pp. 19

[15] **More Tales from the Outer Gulf Islands:** An Anthology of Memories and Anecdotes – British Columbia Historical Association, pp. 24 & 25

[16] **More Tales from the Outer Gulf Islands:** An Anthology of Memories and Anecdotes – British Columbia Historical Association, pp. 24, 25 & 39

[17] **More Tales from the Outer Gulf Islands:** An Anthology of Memories and Anecdotes – British Columbia Historical Association, pp. 24, 25 & 39

[18] **A Gulf Islands Patchwork:** Some Early Events on the Islands of Galiano, Pender, Saturna, North and South Pender – British Columbia Historical Association, pp. 131 and **Homesteads and Snug Harbours:** The Gulf Islands – Peter Murray, pp. 66

[19] **A Self-Guided Historic Tour of the Pender Islands:** The Pender Islands Museum Society, pp. 3

[20] **A Gulf Islands Patchwork:** Some Early Events on the Islands of Galiano, Pender, Saturna, North and South Pender – British Columbia Historical Association, pp. 132

[21] **More Tales from the Outer Gulf Islands:** An Anthology of Memories and Anecdotes – British Columbia Historical Association, pp. 39 & 40 and **Island Heritage Buildings** – Thomas K. Ovanin, Islands Trust, pp. 136

[22] **A Gulf Islands Patchwork:** Some Early Events on the Islands of Galiano, Pender, Saturna, North and South Pender – British Columbia Historical Association, pp. 132

[23] **Hope Bay Store website**

[24] **A Gulf Islands Patchwork:** Some Early Events on the Islands of Galiano, Pender, Saturna, North and South Pender – British Columbia Historical Association, pp. 132

[25] **More Tales from the Outer Gulf Islands:** An Anthology of Memories and Anecdotes – British Columbia Historical Association, pp. 41 and **Island Heritage Buildings** – Thomas K. Ovanin, Islands Trust, pp. 132

[26] **Hope Bay Store website**

[27] **More Tales from the Outer Gulf Islands:** An Anthology of Memories and Anecdotes – British Columbia Historical Association, pp. 40 & 41

[28] **A Self-Guided Historic Tour of the Pender Islands:** The Pender Islands Museum Society, pp. 5

[29] **Homesteads and Snug Harbours:** The Gulf Islands Peter Murray, pp. 69

[30] **A Self-Guided Historic Tour of the Pender Islands:** The Pender Islands Museum Society, pp. 5

[31] **The Lost Heritage of the Penders:** Limited Edition Calendar, 2004 – Pender Islands Museum Society

[32] **More Tales from the Outer Gulf Islands:** An Anthology of Memories and Anecdotes – British Columbia Historical Association, pp. 39, 43 & 44

[33] **The Lost Heritage of the Penders:** Limited Edition Calendar, 2004 – Pender Islands Museum Society

[34] **A Self-Guided Historic Tour of the Pender Islands:** The Pender Islands Museum Society, pp. 5

[35] **More Tales from the Outer Gulf Islands:** An Anthology of Memories and Anecdotes – British Columbia Historical Association, pp. 43 & 44

[36] **More Tales from the Outer Gulf Islands:** An Anthology of Memories and Anecdotes – British Columbia Historical Association, pp. 39, 43 & 44

[37] **More Tales from the Outer Gulf Islands:** An Anthology of Memories and Anecdotes – British Columbia Historical Association, pp. 61-65

[38] **The Lost Heritage of the Penders:** Limited Edition Calendar, 2004 – Pender Islands Museum Society

[39] **A Self-Guided Historic Tour of the Pender Islands:** The Pender Islands Museum Society, pp. 5

[40] **A Self-Guided Historic Tour of the Pender Islands:** The Pender Islands Museum Society, pp. 5 & 13

[41] **More Tales from the Outer Gulf Islands:** An Anthology of Memories and Anecdotes – British Columbia Historical Association, pp. 44 & 117

[42] **Pender Islands Recreation and Agriculture Hall Association newsletter:** Spring 2005

[43] **The Pender Post:** Celebrating the activities of the people of Pender Island at the Millennium, The Pender Post Society, pp. 15

[44] **A Gulf Islands Patchwork:** Some Early Events on the Islands of Galiano, Mayne, Saturna, North and South Pender – British Columbia Historical Association, pp. 105 & 106

[45] **A Gulf Islands Patchwork:** Some Early Events on the Islands of Galiano, Mayne, Saturna, North and South Pender – British Columbia Historical Association, pp. 105 & 106

[46] **A Gulf Islands Patchwork:** Some Early Events on the Islands of Galiano, Mayne, Saturna, North and South Pender – British Columbia Historical Association, pp. 105 & 106

[47] **A Gulf Islands Patchwork:** Some Early Events on the Islands of Galiano, Mayne, Saturna, North and South Pender – British Columbia Historical Association, pp. 101, 105 & 106

[48] **A Gulf Islands Patchwork:** Some Early Events on the Islands of Galiano, Mayne, Saturna, North and South Pender – British Columbia Historical Association, pp. 101, 105 & 106

[49] **A Gulf Islands Patchwork:** Some Early Events on the Islands of Galiano, Mayne, Saturna, North and South Pender – British Columbia Historical Association, pp. 105 & 106

[50] **A Gulf Islands Patchwork:** Some Early Events on the Islands of Galiano, Mayne, Saturna, North and South Pender – British Columbia Historical Association, pp. 23

[51] **Southern Gulf Islands:** An Altitude SuperGuide – Spalding, Montgomery and Pitt, pp. 90 and **Island Heritage Buildings** – Thomas K. Ovanin, Islands Trust, pp. 129

[52] **A Self-Guided Historic Tour of the Pender Islands:** The Pender Islands Museum Society, pp. 13

[53] **The Pender Post:** Celebrating the activities of the people of Pender Island at the Millennium, The Pender Post Society, pp. 85

[54] **More Tales from the Outer Gulf Islands:** An Anthology of Memories and Anecdotes – British Columbia Historical Association, pp. 40 & 104

[55] **More Tales from the Outer Gulf Islands:** An Anthology of Memories and Anecdotes – British Columbia Historical Association, pp. 103-105

[56] **More Tales from the Outer Gulf Islands:** An Anthology of Memories and Anecdotes – British Columbia Historical Association, pp. 103-105

[57] **More Tales from the Outer Gulf Islands:** An Anthology of Memories and Anecdotes – British Columbia Historical Association, pp. 103-105

[58] **More Tales from the Outer Gulf Islands:** An Anthology of Memories and Anecdotes – British Columbia Historical Association, pp. 102-105

[59] **More Tales from the Outer Gulf Islands:** An Anthology of Memories and Anecdotes – British Columbia Historical Association, pp. 103-105

[60] **More Tales from the Outer Gulf Islands:** An Anthology of Memories and Anecdotes – British Columbia Historical Association, pp. 103-105

[61] **More Tales from the Outer Gulf Islands:** An Anthology of Memories and Anecdotes – British Columbia Historical Association, pp. 119 & 120

[62] **A Gulf Islands Patchwork:** Some Early Events on the Islands of Galiano, Mayne, Saturna, North and South Pender – British Columbia Historical Association, pp. 140 and **The Gulf Islanders:** Sound Heritage, Volume V, Number 4, pp. 43 & 44

[63] **Winifred Grey:** A Gentlewoman's Remembrances of Life in England and the Gulf Islands of British Columbia 1871-1910, pp. 113 & 114

[64] **A Gulf Islands Patchwork:** Some Early Events on the Islands of Galiano, Mayne, Saturna, North and South Pender – British Columbia Historical Association, pp. 140 and **The Gulf Islanders:** Sound Heritage, Volume V, Number 4, pp. 44

[65] **A Gulf Islands Patchwork:** Some Early Events on the Islands of Galiano, Mayne, Saturna, North and South Pender – British Columbia Historical Association, pp. 140 and **The Gulf Islanders:** Sound Heritage, Volume V, Number 4, pp. 44

[66] **A Gulf Islands Patchwork:** Some Early Events on the Islands of Galiano, Mayne, Saturna, North and South Pender – British Columbia Historical Association, pp. 140 and **The Gulf Islanders:** Sound Heritage, Volume V, Number 4, pp. 44

[67] **Winifred Grey:** A Gentlewoman's Remembrances of Life in England and the Gulf Islands of British Columbia 1871-1910, pp. 110

[68] **A Gulf Islands Patchwork:** Some Early Events on the Islands of Galiano, Mayne, Saturna, North and South Pender – British Columbia Historical Association, pp. 140 and **The Gulf Islanders:** Sound Heritage, Volume V, Number 4, pp. 44

[69] **More Tales from the Outer Gulf Islands:** An Anthology of Memories and Anecdotes – British Columbia Historical Association, pp. 112-115

[70] **More Tales from the Outer Gulf Islands:** An Anthology of Memories and Anecdotes – British Columbia Historical Association, pp. 112-115

[71] **More Tales from the Outer Gulf Islands:** An Anthology of Memories and Anecdotes – British Columbia Historical Association, pp. 112-115

[72] **More Tales from the Outer Gulf Islands:** An Anthology of Memories and Anecdotes – British Columbia Historical Association, pp. 112-115

[73] **More Tales from the Outer Gulf Islands:** An Anthology of Memories and Anecdotes – British Columbia Historical Association, pp. 112-115

[74] **A Gulf Islands Patchwork:** Some Early Events on the Islands of Galiano, Mayne, Saturna, North and South Pender – British Columbia Historical Association, pp. 130

[75] **A Gulf Islands Patchwork:** Some Early Events on the Islands of Galiano, Mayne, Saturna, North and South Pender – British Columbia Historical Association, pp. 130

[76] **More Tales from the Outer Gulf Islands:** An Anthology of Memories and Anecdotes – British Columbia Historical Association, pp. 74-76

[77] **The Pender Post**: Celebrating the activities of the people of Pender Island at the Millennium, The Pender Post Society, pp. 53

[78] **More Tales from the Outer Gulf Islands:** An Anthology of Memories and Anecdotes – British Columbia Historical Association, pp. 81-83

[79] **More Tales from the Outer Gulf Islands:** An Anthology of Memories and Anecdotes – British Columbia Historical Association, pp. 81-83

[80] **More Tales from the Outer Gulf Islands:** An Anthology of Memories and Anecdotes – British Columbia Historical Association, pp. 81-83

[81] **The Pender Post**: Celebrating the activities of the people of Pender Island at the Millennium, The Pender Post Society, pp. 51

[82] **Southern Gulf Islands**: An Altitude SuperGuide – Spalding, Montgomery and Pitt, pp. 81 & 96

[83] **The Lost Heritage of the Penders:** Limited Edition Calendar, 2004 – Pender Islands Museum Society

[84] **More Tales from the Outer Gulf Islands:** An Anthology of Memories and Anecdotes – British Columbia Historical Association, pp. 45 & 66-68 and **A Self-Guided Historic Tour of the Pender Islands:** The Pender Islands Museum Society, pp. 11

[85] **More Tales from the Outer Gulf Islands:** An Anthology of Memories and Anecdotes – British Columbia Historical Association, pp. 66-68

[86] **A Self-Guided Historic Tour of the Pender Islands:** The Pender Islands Museum Society, pp. 11

[87] **More Tales from the Outer Gulf Islands:** An Anthology of Memories and Anecdotes – British Columbia Historical Association, pp. 68

[88] **More Tales from the Outer Gulf Islands:** An Anthology of Memories and Anecdotes – British Columbia Historical Association, pp. 66-68

[89] **The Gulf Islands Explorer:** The Complete Guide – Bruce Obee, pp. 122

[90] **Island Heritage Buildings** – Thomas K. Ovanin, Islands Trust, pp. 140

[91] **Island Heritage Buildings** – Thomas K. Ovanin, Islands Trust, pp. 140

[92] **Island Heritage Buildings** – Thomas K. Ovanin, Islands Trust, pp. 140

[93] **Island Heritage Buildings** – Thomas K. Ovanin, Islands Trust, pp. 140

[94] **A Self-Guided Historic Tour of the Pender Islands:** The Pender Islands Museum Society, pp. 3

[95] **A Self-Guided Historic Tour of the Pender Islands:** The Pender Islands Museum Society, pp. 3

[96] **Homesteads and Snug Harbours:** The Gulf Islands – Peter Murray, pp. 74

[97] **A Gulf Islands Patchwork:** Some Early Events on the Islands of Galiano, Mayne, Saturna, North and South Pender – British Columbia Historical Association, pp. 35

[98] **Between The Isles:** Life in the Canadian Gulf Islands - Cy Porter, pp. 171

[99] **Island Tides Newspaper:** Volume 16, Number 23, pp. 1

[100] **A Gulf Islands Patchwork:** Some Early Events on the Islands of Galiano, Mayne, Saturna, North and South Pender – British Columbia Historical Association, pp. 35 and **Southern Gulf Islands**: An Altitude SuperGuide – Spalding, Montgomery and Pitt, pp. 95

[101] **More Tales from the Outer Gulf Islands:** An Anthology of Memories and Anecdotes – British Columbia Historical Association, pp. 72 & 73

[102] **A Gulf Islands Patchwork:** Some Early Events on the Islands of Galiano, Mayne, Saturna, North and South Pender – British Columbia Historical Association, pp. 79, 127 & 169

[103] **The Terror Of The Coast:** Land Alienation And Colonial War On Vancouver Island And The Gulf Islands – Chris Arnett, pp. 113

[104] **A Gulf Islands Patchwork:** Some Early Events on the Islands of Galiano, Mayne, Saturna, North and South Pender – British Columbia Historical Association, pp. 79, 127 & 169

[105] **A Gulf Islands Patchwork:** Some Early Events on the Islands of Galiano, Mayne, Saturna, North and South Pender – British Columbia Historical Association, pp. 169 & 170

[106] **A Gulf Islands Patchwork:** Some Early Events on the Islands of Galiano, Mayne, Saturna, North and South Pender – British Columbia Historical Association, pp. 169 & 170

[107] **A Gulf Islands Patchwork:** Some Early Events on the Islands of Galiano, Mayne, Saturna, North and South Pender – British Columbia Historical Association, pp. 169 & 170

[108] **More Tales from the Outer Gulf Islands:** An Anthology of Memories and Anecdotes – British Columbia Historical Association, pp. 55

[109] **The Historical Pender Islands:** Limited Edition Calendar, 2006 – Pender Islands Museum Society

[110] **Mayne Island & The Outer Gulf Islands**: A History – Marie Elliott, pp. 82

[111] **Island Tides Newspaper:** Volume 16, Number 23, pp. 1

[112] **More Tales from the Outer Gulf Islands:** An Anthology of Memories and Anecdotes – British Columbia Historical Association, pp. 55

[113] **Southern Gulf Islands**: An Altitude SuperGuide – Spalding, Montgomery and Pitt, pp. 94

[114] **Hope Bay Store website**

[115] **A Self-Guided Historic Tour of the Pender Islands:** The Pender Islands Museum Society, pp. 3

[116] **Island Heritage Buildings** – Thomas K. Ovanin, Islands Trust, pp. 131

[117] **Homesteads and Snug Harbours:** The Gulf Islands – Peter Murray, pp. 67

[118] **Hope Bay Store website**

[119] **Homesteads and Snug Harbours:** The Gulf Islands – Peter Murray, pp. 67

[120] **A Gulf Islands Patchwork:** Some Early Events on the Islands of Galiano, Pender, Saturna, North and South Pender – British Columbia Historical Association, pp. 96

[121] **Hope Bay Store website**

[122] **Hope Bay Store website**

[123] **Hope Bay Store website**

[124] **Hope Bay Store website**

[125] **Island Heritage Buildings** – Thomas K. Ovanin, Islands Trust, pp. 132

[126] **Hope Bay Store website**

[127] **Hope Bay Store website**

[128] **A Gulf Islands Patchwork:** Some Early Events on the Islands of Galiano, Mayne, Saturna, North and South Pender – British Columbia Historical Association, pp. 96

[129] **A Gulf Islands Patchwork:** Some Early Events on the Islands of Galiano, Mayne, Saturna, North and South Pender – British Columbia Historical Association, pp. 100

[130] **More Tales from the Outer Gulf Islands:** An Anthology of Memories and Anecdotes – British Columbia Historical Association, pp. 24-31

[131] **More Tales from the Outer Gulf Islands:** An Anthology of Memories and Anecdotes – British Columbia Historical Association, pp. 24-31

[132] **More Tales from the Outer Gulf Islands:** An Anthology of Memories and Anecdotes – British Columbia Historical Association, pp. 30 & 31

[133] **More Tales from the Outer Gulf Islands:** An Anthology of Memories and Anecdotes – British Columbia Historical Association, pp. 31

[134] **More Tales from the Outer Gulf Islands:** An Anthology of Memories and Anecdotes – British Columbia Historical Association, pp. 29, 31 & 40

[135] **A Gulf Islands Patchwork:** Some Early Events on the Islands of Galiano, Mayne, Saturna, North and South Pender – British Columbia Historical Association, pp. 161

[136] **More Tales from the Outer Gulf Islands:** An Anthology of Memories and Anecdotes – British Columbia Historical Association, pp. 29

[137] **More Tales from the Outer Gulf Islands:** An Anthology of Memories and Anecdotes – British Columbia Historical Association, pp. 32

[138] **More Tales from the Outer Gulf Islands:** An Anthology of Memories and Anecdotes – British Columbia Historical Association, pp. 33

[139] **More Tales from the Outer Gulf Islands:** An Anthology of Memories and Anecdotes – British Columbia Historical Association, pp. 21 & 25

[140] **A Gulf Islands Patchwork:** Some Early Events on the Islands of Galiano, Mayne, Saturna, North and South Pender – British Columbia Historical Association, pp. 114-116

[141] **A Gulf Islands Patchwork:** Some Early Events on the Islands of Galiano, Mayne, Saturna, North and South Pender – British Columbia Historical Association, pp. 114-116

[142] **A Gulf Islands Patchwork:** Some Early Events on the Islands of Galiano, Mayne, Saturna, North and South Pender – British Columbia Historical Association, pp. 114-116

[143] **A Self-Guided Historic Tour of the Pender Islands:** The Pender Islands Museum Society, pp. 3

[144] **The Pender Post:** Celebrating the activities of the people of Pender Island at the Millennium, The Pender Post Society, pp. 19

[145] **A Self-Guided Historic Tour of the Pender Islands:** The Pender Islands Museum Society, pp. 3

[146] **A Gulf Islands Patchwork:** Some Early Events on the Islands of Galiano, Mayne, Saturna, North and South Pender – British Columbia Historical Association, pp. 117

[147] **A Gulf Islands Patchwork:** Some Early Events on the Islands of Galiano, Mayne, Saturna, North and South Pender – British Columbia Historical Association, pp. 117

[148] **A Gulf Islands Patchwork:** Some Early Events on the Islands of Galiano, Mayne, Saturna, North and South Pender – British Columbia Historical Association, pp. 117

[149] **A Self-Guided Historic Tour of the Pender Islands:** The Pender Islands Museum Society, pp. 13

[150] **A Gulf Islands Patchwork:** Some Early Events on the Islands of Galiano, Mayne, Saturna, North and South Pender – British Columbia Historical Association, pp. 117

[151] **A Gulf Islands Patchwork:** Some Early Events on the Islands of Galiano, Mayne, Saturna, North and South Pender – British Columbia Historical Association, pp. 21 & 107

[152] **More Tales from the Outer Gulf Islands:** An Anthology of Memories and Anecdotes – British Columbia Historical Association, pp. 39

[153] **A Gulf Islands Patchwork:** Some Early Events on the Islands of Galiano, Mayne, Saturna, North and South Pender – British Columbia Historical Association, pp. 21 & 107

[154] **A Gulf Islands Patchwork:** Some Early Events on the Islands of Galiano, Mayne, Saturna, North and South Pender – British Columbia Historical Association, pp. 107

[155] **A Gulf Islands Patchwork:** Some Early Events on the Islands of Galiano, Mayne, Saturna, North and South Pender – British Columbia Historical Association, pp. 109 & 162

[156] **A Gulf Islands Patchwork:** Some Early Events on the Islands of Galiano, Mayne, Saturna, North and South Pender – British Columbia Historical Association, pp. 107 & 111

[157] **A Self-Guided Historic Tour of the Pender Islands:** The Pender Islands Museum Society, pp. 13

[158] **More Tales from the Outer Gulf Islands:** An Anthology of Memories and Anecdotes – British Columbia Historical Association, pp. 37 & 38

[159] **More Tales from the Outer Gulf Islands:** An Anthology of Memories and Anecdotes – British Columbia Historical Association, pp. 37 & 38

[160] **More Tales from the Outer Gulf Islands:** An Anthology of Memories and Anecdotes – British Columbia Historical Association, pp. 37 & 38 and **A Gulf Islands Patchwork:** Some Early Events on the Islands of Galiano, Mayne, Saturna, North and South Pender – British Columbia Historical Association, pp. 101

[161] **More Tales from the Outer Gulf Islands:** An Anthology of Memories and Anecdotes – British Columbia Historical Association, pp. 37 & 38

[162] **British Colunbia Historical News:** Volume 37 Number 2

[163] **British Colunbia Historical News:** Volume 37 Number 2

[164] **Gulf Islands National Park Reserve of Canada website**: Visitor Information, Parks Canada

[165] **The Lost Heritage of the Penders:** Limited Edition Calendar, 2004 – Pender Islands Museum Society

[166] **A Gulf Islands Patchwork:** Some Early Events on the Islands of Galiano, Mayne, Saturna, North and South Pender – British Columbia Historical Association, pp. 112-113

[167] **A Gulf Islands Patchwork:** Some Early Events on the Islands of Galiano, Mayne, Saturna, North and South Pender – British Columbia Historical Association, pp. 112-113

[168] **A Gulf Islands Patchwork:** Some Early Events on the Islands of Galiano, Mayne, Saturna, North and South Pender – British Columbia Historical Association, pp. 112-113

[169] **More Tales from the Outer Gulf Islands:** An Anthology of Memories and Anecdotes – British Columbia Historical Association, pp. 39-41 and **Island Heritage Buildings** – Thomas K. Ovanin, Islands Trust, pp. 136

[170] **More Tales from the Outer Gulf Islands:** An Anthology of Memories and Anecdotes – British Columbia Historical Association, pp. 39-41

[171] **More Tales from the Outer Gulf Islands:** An Anthology of Memories and Anecdotes – British Columbia Historical Association, pp. 40

[172] **More Tales from the Outer Gulf Islands:** An Anthology of Memories and Anecdotes – British Columbia Historical Association, pp. 39-41 & 103-105

[173] **More Tales from the Outer Gulf Islands:** An Anthology of Memories and Anecdotes – British Columbia Historical Association, pp. 41

[174] **A Self-Guided Historic Tour of the Pender Islands:** The Pender Islands Museum Society, pp. 7

[175] **A Gulf Islands Patchwork:** Some Early Events on the Islands of Galiano, Mayne, Saturna, North and South Pender – British Columbia Historical Association, pp. 31 & 32

[176] **A Gulf Islands Patchwork:** Some Early Events on the Islands of Galiano, Mayne, Saturna, North and South Pender – British Columbia Historical Association, pp. 31 & 32

[177] **The Pender Post:** Celebrating the activities of the people of Pender Island at the Millennium, The Pender Post Society, pp. 11

[178] **More Tales from the Outer Gulf Islands:** An Anthology of Memories and Anecdotes – British Columbia Historical Association, pp. 100

[179] **Island Heritage Buildings** – Thomas K. Ovanin, Islands Trust, pp. 128

[180] **Island Heritage Buildings** – Thomas K. Ovanin, Islands Trust, pp. 128

[181] **Island Heritage Buildings** – Thomas K. Ovanin, Islands Trust, pp. 128

[182] **Island Heritage Buildings** – Thomas K. Ovanin, Islands Trust, pp. 128

[183] **The Pioneers of the Penders:** Limited Edition Calendar, 2005 – Pender Islands Museum Society

[184] **Island Heritage Buildings** – Thomas K. Ovanin, Islands Trust, pp. 132

[185] **Island Heritage Buildings** – Thomas K. Ovanin, Islands Trust, pp. 132

[186] **Island Heritage Buildings** – Thomas K. Ovanin, Islands Trust, pp. 132

[187] **More Tales from the Outer Gulf Islands:** An Anthology of Memories and Anecdotes – British Columbia Historical Association, pp. 74

[188] **Southern Gulf Islands:** An Altitude SuperGuide – Spalding, Montgomery and Pitt, pp. 90

[189] **A Gulf Islands Patchwork:** Some Early Events on the Islands of Galiano, Mayne, Saturna, North and South Pender – British Columbia Historical Association, pp. 159

[190] **A Gulf Islands Patchwork:** Some Early Events on the Islands of Galiano, Mayne, Saturna, North and South Pender – British Columbia Historical Association, pp. 159

[191] **More Tales from the Outer Gulf Islands:** An Anthology of Memories and Anecdotes – British Columbia Historical Association, pp. 116

[192] **Pender Island Volunteer Firefighter's Association website**

[193] **A Gulf Islands Patchwork:** Some Early Events on the Islands of Galiano, Mayne, Saturna, North and South Pender – British Columbia Historical Association, pp. 108 & 109

[194] **A Gulf Islands Patchwork:** Some Early Events on the Islands of Galiano, Mayne, Saturna, North and South Pender – British Columbia Historical Association, pp. 108 & 109

[195] **More Tales from the Outer Gulf Islands:** An Anthology of Memories and Anecdotes – British Columbia Historical Association, pp. 61-65

[196] **More Tales from the Outer Gulf Islands:** An Anthology of Memories and Anecdotes – British Columbia Historical Association, pp. 61-65

[197] **More Tales from the Outer Gulf Islands:** An Anthology of Memories and Anecdotes – British Columbia Historical Association, pp. 64

[198] **More Tales from the Outer Gulf Islands:** An Anthology of Memories and Anecdotes – British Columbia Historical Association, pp. 61-65

[199] **More Tales from the Outer Gulf Islands:** An Anthology of Memories and Anecdotes – British Columbia Historical Association, pp. 61-65

[200] **More Tales from the Outer Gulf Islands:** An Anthology of Memories and Anecdotes – British Columbia Historical Association, pp. 78-80

[201] **More Tales from the Outer Gulf Islands:** An Anthology of Memories and Anecdotes – British Columbia Historical Association, pp. 78-80

[202] **More Tales from the Outer Gulf Islands:** An Anthology of Memories and Anecdotes – British Columbia Historical Association, pp. 78-80

[203] **More Tales from the Outer Gulf Islands:** An Anthology of Memories and Anecdotes – British Columbia Historical Association, pp. 78-80

[204] **More Tales from the Outer Gulf Islands:** An Anthology of Memories and Anecdotes – British Columbia Historical Association, pp. 78-80

[205] **Island Tides Newspaper:** Volume 17, Number 13, pp. 1

[206] **Mayne Island & The Outer Gulf Islands**: A History – Marie Elliott, pp. 96

[207] **Southern Gulf Islands**: An Altitude SuperGuide – Spalding, Montgomery and Pitt, pp. 30

[208] **Southern Gulf Islands**: An Altitude SuperGuide – Spalding, Montgomery and Pitt, pp. 30

[209] **Community Parks Guide:** Pender Islands Parks Commission, pp. 21

[210] **A Gulf Islands Patchwork:** Some Early Events on the Islands of Galiano, Pender, Saturna, North and South Pender – British Columbia Historical Association, pp. 36

[211] **A Gulf Islands Patchwork:** Some Early Events on the Islands of Galiano, Pender, Saturna, North and South Pender – British Columbia Historical Association, pp. 36 & 150

[212] **Winifred Grey:** A Gentlewoman's Remembrances of Life in England and the Gulf Islands of British Columbia 1871-1910, pp. 113

[213] **Homesteads and Snug Harbours:** The Gulf Islands – Peter Murray, pp. 73

[214] **Homesteads and Snug Harbours:** The Gulf Islands – Peter Murray, pp. 72

[215] **A Gulf Islands Patchwork:** Some Early Events on the Islands of Galiano, Pender, Saturna, North and South Pender – British Columbia Historical Association, pp. 36

[216] **A Gulf Islands Patchwork:** Some Early Events on the Islands of Galiano, Mayne, Saturna, North and South Pender – British Columbia Historical Association, pp. 169-171

[217] **A Gulf Islands Patchwork:** Some Early Events on the Islands of Galiano, Mayne, Saturna, North and South Pender – British Columbia Historical Association, pp. 169-171

[218] **More Tales from the Outer Gulf Islands:** An Anthology of Memories and Anecdotes – British Columbia Historical Association, pp. 47-49 and **A Gulf Islands Patchwork:** Some Early Events on the Islands of Galiano, Pender, Saturna, North and South Pender – British Columbia Historical Association, pp. 170 & 171

[219] **A Gulf Islands Patchwork:** Some Early Events on the Islands of Galiano, Mayne, Saturna, North and South Pender – British Columbia Historical Association, pp. 170 & 171 and **More Tales from the Outer Gulf Islands:** An Anthology of Memories and Anecdotes – British Columbia Historical Association, pp. 47 and **Homesteads and Snug Harbours:** The Gulf Islands – Peter Murray, pp. 71

[220] **A Gulf Islands Patchwork:** Some Early Events on the Islands of Galiano, Mayne, Saturna, North and South Pender – British Columbia Historical Association, pp. 170 & 171 and **More Tales from the Outer Gulf Islands:** An Anthology of Memories and Anecdotes – British Columbia Historical Association, pp. 47 and **Homesteads and Snug Harbours:** The Gulf Islands – Peter Murray, pp. 71

[221] **A Gulf Islands Patchwork:** Some Early Events on the Islands of Galiano, Pender, Saturna, North and South Pender – British Columbia Historical Association, pp. 170 & 171 and **More Tales from the Outer Gulf Islands:** An Anthology of Memories and Anecdotes – British Columbia Historical Association, pp. 48

[222] **Homesteads and Snug Harbours:** The Gulf Islands – Peter Murray, pp. 67

[223] **A Gulf Islands Patchwork:** Some Early Events on the Islands of Galiano, Mayne, Saturna, North and South Pender – British Columbia Historical Association, pp. 186

[224] **A Self-Guided Historic Tour of the Pender Islands:** The Pender Islands Museum Society, pp. 1

[225] **Homesteads and Snug Harbours:** The Gulf Islands – Peter Murray, pp. 67

[226] **A Gulf Islands Patchwork:** Some Early Events on the Islands of Galiano, Mayne, Saturna, North and South Pender – British Columbia Historical Association, pp. 118 & 186

[227] **A Gulf Islands Patchwork:** Some Early Events on the Islands of Galiano, Mayne, Saturna, North and South Pender – British Columbia Historical Association, pp. 118 & 186

[228] **A Gulf Islands Patchwork:** Some Early Events on the Islands of Galiano, Mayne, Saturna, North and South Pender – British Columbia Historical Association, pp. 118 & 186

[229] **Homesteads and Snug Harbours:** The Gulf Islands – Peter Murray, pp. 67

[230] **The Gulf Islands Explorer:** The Complete Guide – Bruce Obee, pp. 125

[231] **A Gulf Islands Patchwork:** Some Early Events on the Islands of Galiano, Mayne, Saturna, North and South Pender – British Columbia Historical Association, pp. 38

[232] **A Gulf Islands Patchwork:** Some Early Events on the Islands of Galiano, Mayne, Saturna, North and South Pender – British Columbia Historical Association, pp. 38

[233] **Southern Gulf Islands**: An Altitude SuperGuide – Spalding, Montgomery and Pitt, pp. 21

[234] **A Gulf Islands Patchwork:** Some Early Events on the Islands of Galiano, Mayne, Saturna, North and South Pender – British Columbia Historical Association, pp. 125

[235] **A Gulf Islands Patchwork:** Some Early Events on the Islands of Galiano, Mayne, Saturna, North and South Pender – British Columbia Historical Association, pp. 125 & 126

[236] **A Gulf Islands Patchwork:** Some Early Events on the Islands of Galiano, Mayne, Saturna, North and South Pender – British Columbia Historical Association, pp. 125

[237] **Gulf Islands National Park Reserve of Canada website**: Visitor Information, Parks Canada

[238] **A Gulf Islands Patchwork:** Some Early Events on the Islands of Galiano, Mayne, Saturna, North and South Pender – British Columbia Historical Association, pp. 33

[239] **More Tales from the Outer Gulf Islands:** An Anthology of Memories and Anecdotes – British Columbia Historical Association, pp. 146

[240] **A Gulf Islands Patchwork:** Some Early Events on the Islands of Galiano, Mayne, Saturna, North and South Pender – British Columbia Historical Association, pp. 33

[241] **A Gulf Islands Patchwork:** Some Early Events on the Islands of Galiano, Mayne, Saturna, North and South Pender – British Columbia Historical Association, pp. 33

[242] **The Lost Heritage of the Penders:** Limited Edition Calendar, 2004 – Pender Islands Museum Society

[243] **The Lost Heritage of the Penders:** Limited Edition Calendar, 2004 – Pender Islands Museum Society

[244] **The Gulf Islands Explorer:** The Complete Guide – Bruce Obee, pp. 114

[245] **Homesteads and Snug Harbours:** The Gulf Islands – Peter Murray, pp. 74

[246] **A Gulf Islands Patchwork:** Some Early Events on the Islands of Galiano, Mayne, Saturna, North and South Pender – British Columbia Historical Association, pp. 5 & 171

[247] **A Gulf Islands Patchwork:** Some Early Events on the Islands of Galiano, Mayne, Saturna, North and South Pender – British Columbia Historical Association, pp. 5 & 171

[248] **A Gulf Islands Patchwork:** Some Early Events on the Islands of Galiano, Mayne, Saturna, North and South Pender – British Columbia Historical Association, pp. 5

[249] **A Gulf Islands Patchwork:** Some Early Events on the Islands of Galiano, Mayne, Saturna, North and South Pender – British Columbia Historical Association, pp. 172 & 173

[250] **A Gulf Islands Patchwork:** Some Early Events on the Islands of Galiano, Mayne, Saturna, North and South Pender – British Columbia Historical Association, pp. 172 & 173

[251] **A Gulf Islands Patchwork:** Some Early Events on the Islands of Galiano, Mayne, Saturna, North and South Pender – British Columbia Historical Association, pp. 172 & 173

[252] **Southern Gulf Islands**: An Altitude SuperGuide – Spalding, Montgomery and Pitt, pp. 232

[253] **A Gulf Islands Patchwork:** Some Early Events on the Islands of Galiano, Mayne, Saturna, North and South Pender – British Columbia Historical Association, pp. 172 & 173

[254] **A Self-Guided Historic Tour of the Pender Islands:** The Pender Islands Museum Society, pp. 15

[255] **Homesteads and Snug Harbours:** The Gulf Islands – Peter Murray, pp. 68

[256] **A Gulf Islands Patchwork:** Some Early Events on the Islands of Galiano, Mayne, Saturna, North and South Pender – British Columbia Historical Association, pp. 66 & 67

[257] **A Gulf Islands Patchwork:** Some Early Events on the Islands of Galiano, Mayne, Saturna, North and South Pender – British Columbia Historical Association, pp. 66 & 67

[258] **Island Heritage Buildings** – Thomas K. Ovanin, Islands Trust, pp. 133

[259] **More Tales from the Outer Gulf Islands:** An Anthology of Memories and Anecdotes – British Columbia Historical Association, pp. 23

[260] **More Tales from the Outer Gulf Islands:** An Anthology of Memories and Anecdotes – British Columbia Historical Association, pp. 23

[261] **More Tales from the Outer Gulf Islands:** An Anthology of Memories and Anecdotes – British Columbia Historical Association, pp. 23

[262] **More Tales from the Outer Gulf Islands:** An Anthology of Memories and Anecdotes – British Columbia Historical Association, pp. 23 & 24

[263] **More Tales from the Outer Gulf Islands:** An Anthology of Memories and Anecdotes – British Columbia Historical Association, pp. 24 & 25

[264] **A Gulf Islands Patchwork:** Some Early Events on the Islands of Galiano, Mayne, Saturna, North and South Pender – British Columbia Historical Association, pp. 20, 21 & 124

[265] **A Gulf Islands Patchwork:** Some Early Events on the Islands of Galiano, Mayne, Saturna, North and South Pender – British Columbia Historical Association, pp. 20 & 21

[266] **Homesteads and Snug Harbours:** The Gulf Islands – Peter Murray, pp. 64

[267] **Homesteads and Snug Harbours:** The Gulf Islands – Peter Murray, pp. 64

[268] **Island Heritage Buildings** – Thomas K. Ovanin, Islands Trust, pp. 139

[269] **Island Heritage Buildings** – Thomas K. Ovanin, Islands Trust, pp. 139

[270] **The Gulf Islanders:** Sound Heritage, Volume V, Number 4, pp. 57 & 58

[271] **Homesteads and Snug Harbours:** The Gulf Islands – Peter Murray, pp. 64

[272] **A Gulf Islands Patchwork:** Some Early Events on the Islands of Galiano, Mayne, Saturna, North and South Pender – British Columbia Historical Association, pp. 39, 68 & 125

[273] **A Gulf Islands Patchwork:** Some Early Events on the Islands of Galiano, Mayne, Saturna, North and South Pender – British Columbia Historical Association, pp. 39, 40, 123, 128 & 129

[274] **The Gulf Islanders:** Sound Heritage, Volume V, Number 4, pp. 39 and **A Gulf Islands Patchwork:** Some Early Events on the Islands of Galiano, Mayne, Saturna, North and South Pender – British Columbia Historical Association, pp. 128 & 129

[275] **The Gulf Islanders:** Sound Heritage, Volume V, Number 4, pp. 39 and **A Gulf Islands Patchwork:** Some Early Events on the Islands of Galiano, Mayne, Saturna, North and South Pender – British Columbia Historical Association, pp. 128 & 129

[276] **The Gulf Islanders:** Sound Heritage, Volume V, Number 4, pp. 39 and **A Gulf Islands Patchwork:** Some Early Events on the Islands of Galiano, Mayne, Saturna, North and South Pender – British Columbia Historical Association, pp. 128 & 129

[277] **The Gulf Islanders:** Sound Heritage, Volume V, Number 4, pp. 39 and **A Gulf Islands Patchwork:** Some Early Events on the Islands of Galiano, Mayne, Saturna, North and South Pender – British Columbia Historical Association, pp. 128 & 129

[278] **A Gulf Islands Patchwork:** Some Early Events on the Islands of Galiano, Mayne, Saturna, North and South Pender – British Columbia Historical Association, pp. 68

[279] **More Tales from the Outer Gulf Islands:** An Anthology of Memories and Anecdotes – British Columbia Historical Association, pp. 26 & 35

[280] **More Tales from the Outer Gulf Islands:** An Anthology of Memories and Anecdotes – British Columbia Historical Association, pp. 26 & 35

[281] **More Tales from the Outer Gulf Islands:** An Anthology of Memories and Anecdotes – British Columbia Historical Association, pp. 26 & 35

[282] **More Tales from the Outer Gulf Islands:** An Anthology of Memories and Anecdotes – British Columbia Historical Association, pp. 26 & 35

[283] **More Tales from the Outer Gulf Islands:** An Anthology of Memories and Anecdotes – British Columbia Historical Association, pp. 26 & 35

[284] **A Gulf Islands Patchwork:** Some Early Events on the Islands of Galiano, Mayne, Saturna, North and South Pender – British Columbia Historical Association, pp. 97 & 98

[285] **More Tales from the Outer Gulf Islands:** An Anthology of Memories and Anecdotes – British Columbia Historical Association, pp. 26 & 35

[286] **More Tales from the Outer Gulf Islands:** An Anthology of Memories and Anecdotes – British Columbia Historical Association, pp. 45 & 46

[287] **A Self-Guided Historic Tour of the Pender Islands:** The Pender Islands Museum Society, pp. 11

[288] **A Self-Guided Historic Tour of the Pender Islands:** The Pender Islands Museum Society, pp. 11

[289] **More Tales from the Outer Gulf Islands:** An Anthology of Memories and Anecdotes – British Columbia Historical Association, pp. 45 & 46

[290] **More Tales from the Outer Gulf Islands:** An Anthology of Memories and Anecdotes – British Columbia Historical Association, pp. 45 & 46

[291] **More Tales from the Outer Gulf Islands:** An Anthology of Memories and Anecdotes – British Columbia Historical Association, pp. 45 & 46

[292] **A Gulf Islands Patchwork:** Some Early Events on the Islands of Galiano, Mayne, Saturna, North and South Pender – British Columbia Historical Association, pp. 36

[293] **Homesteads and Snug Harbours:** The Gulf Islands – Peter Murray, pp. 55

[294] **A Gulf Islands Patchwork:** Some Early Events on the Islands of Galiano, Mayne, Saturna, North and South Pender – British Columbia Historical Association, pp. 36

[295] **Southern Gulf Islands:** An Altitude SuperGuide – Spalding, Montgomery and Pitt, pp. 30 & 97

[296] **Homesteads and Snug Harbours:** The Gulf Islands – Peter Murray, pp. 64

[297] **The Historical Pender Islands:** Limited Edition Calendar, 2006 – Pender Islands Museum Society

[298] **More Tales from the Outer Gulf Islands:** An Anthology of Memories and Anecdotes – British Columbia Historical Association, pp. 37 & 38

[299] **A Gulf Islands Patchwork:** Some Early Events on the Islands of Galiano, Mayne, Saturna, North and South Pender – British Columbia Historical Association, pp. 101

[300] **A Gulf Islands Patchwork:** Some Early Events on the Islands of Galiano, Mayne, Saturna, North and South Pender – British Columbia Historical Association, pp. 43-44

[301] **Homesteads and Snug Harbours:** The Gulf Islands – Peter Murray, pp. 69

[302] **The Historical Pender Islands:** Limited Edition Calendar, 2006 – Pender Islands Museum Society

[303] **A Gulf Islands Patchwork:** Some Early Events on the Islands of Galiano, Mayne, Saturna, North and South Pender – British Columbia Historical Association, pp. 43-44 and **The Historical Pender Islands:** Limited Edition Calendar, 2006 – Pender Islands Museum Society

[304] **A Gulf Islands Patchwork:** Some Early Events on the Islands of Galiano, Mayne, Saturna, North and South Pender – British Columbia Historical Association, pp. 171

[305] **A Gulf Islands Patchwork:** Some Early Events on the Islands of Galiano, Mayne, Saturna, North and South Pender – British Columbia Historical Association, maps

[306] **A Gulf Islands Patchwork:** Some Early Events on the Islands of Galiano, Mayne, Saturna, North and South Pender – British Columbia Historical Association, pp. 69 & 70

[307] **A Gulf Islands Patchwork:** Some Early Events on the Islands of Galiano, Mayne, Saturna, North and South Pender – British Columbia Historical Association, pp. 69 & 70

[308] **A Gulf Islands Patchwork:** Some Early Events on the Islands of Galiano, Mayne, Saturna, North and South Pender – British Columbia Historical Association, pp. 69 & 70

[309] **A Gulf Islands Patchwork:** Some Early Events on the Islands of Galiano, Mayne, Saturna, North and South Pender – British Columbia Historical Association, pp. 127

[310] **Southern Gulf Islands:** An Altitude SuperGuide – Spalding, Montgomery and Pitt, pp. 96

[311] **MayneLiner Magazine:** Volume 15, Number 8, pp. 20

[312] **City of Placerville, California website**

[313] **Plants of the Pacific Northwest Coast:** Washington, Oregon, British Columbia and Alaska
[314] **Plants of the Pacific Northwest Coast:** Washington, Oregon, British Columbia and Alaska

Index